Kate and Emily's
GUIDE TO
SINGLE
PARENTING

Kate and Emily's
GUIDE TO
SINGLE
PARENTING

Kate Ford and Emily Abbott

HAY HOUSE

Australia • Canada • Hong Kong • India
South Africa • United Kingdom • United States

First published and distributed in the United Kingdom by:
Hay House UK Ltd, 292B Kensal Rd, London W10 5BE.
Tel.: (44) 20 8962 1230; Fax: (44) 20 8962 1239. www.hayhouse.co.uk

Published and distributed in the United States of America by:
Hay House, Inc., PO Box 5100, Carlsbad, CA 92018-5100.
Tel.: (1) 760 431 7695 or (800) 654 5126; Fax: (1) 760 431 6948 or (800) 650 5115.
www.hayhouse.com

Published and distributed in Australia by:
Hay House Australia Ltd, 18/36 Ralph St, Alexandria NSW 2015.
Tel.: (61) 2 9669 4299; Fax: (61) 2 9669 4144. www.hayhouse.com.au

Published and distributed in the Republic of South Africa by:
Hay House SA (Pty), Ltd, PO Box 990, Witkoppen 2068.
Tel./Fax: (27) 11 467 8904. www.hayhouse.co.za

Published and distributed in India by:
Hay House Publishers India, Muskaan Complex,
Plot No.3, B-2, Vasant Kunj, New Delhi – 110 070.
Tel.: (91) 11 4176 1620; Fax: (91) 11 4176 1630. www.hayhouse.co.in

Distributed in Canada by:
Raincoast, 9050 Shaughnessy St, Vancouver, BC V6P 6E5.
Tel.: (1) 604 323 7100; Fax: (1) 604 323 2600

© Kate Ford and Emily Abbott, 2008

Design and layout by e-Digital Design.

The moral rights of the authors have been asserted.

The authors of this book do not dispense medical advice or prescribe the use of any
technique as a form of treatment for physical or medical problems without the advice of
a physician, either directly or indirectly. The intent of the authors is only to offer information of a general nature to help you in your quest for emotional and spiritual wellbeing.
In the event you use any of the information in this book for yourself, which is your con-
stitutional right, the authors and the publisher assume no responsibility for your actions.

A catalogue record for this book is available from the British Library.

ISBN 978-1-4019-1610-7

Printed in the UK by CPI William Clowes Beccles NR34 7TL

CONTENTS

DEDICATION

We'd like to dedicate this book to all the single parents we have met along the way who have turned the Kate and Emily experience into the most amazing journey of learning, passion and laughs - you are all in this book somewhere. A special mention to Dee and Cara, the non-single parents who have gone more than the extra mile for us!

Kate would like to dedicate her half to her friends and family who have put up with and supported the highs and lows (and still continue to). But most of all... to the best girl and boy in the whole world, Alice and George. All my love, Mummy xxx

Emily would like to dedicate her half to Imo and Archie, pets, family and friends - you know who you are. Thank you! Love, Em xxx

Chapter 1

WE'RE SINGLE PARENTS WHO CAN HELP YOU AND YOUR FAMILY THROUGH THIS MAZE

We're Kate and Emily, two regular folk who have found ourselves single parents. To this day we're still both utterly amazed that we're part of this group. We hate being defined or even described as 'single parents', however we *are*, and we think that recognizing this fact has been pretty important when it comes to dealing with our new lives.

If You Were Left or If You Did the Leaving We'll Help You Grab Your Future

Down to the nitty-gritty: Emily left a surprised and devastated husband and Kate was surprised and devastated when left. These different experiences provide a great balance and help us to understand issues from different perspectives. Whichever gang you're in (dumper or dumpee), we do know that arriving at the point where you're reading this book will have been difficult, both for you and your children. So we hope to offer a practical and positive take on life to help you and your family move onwards and upwards. At the end of the day nothing's happened that's not worth trying to get over and move on from, and (we assume) there is no REAL reason why your children should be deprived of someone they need enormously – their dad. Helping you get to the point where you realize this and can fully embrace the future is what 'Kate and Emily' and this book are all about.

You May Feel Your Story Is Unique, but We Can See the Similarities

When people say 'It's different for me because my circumstances are not the same as yours,' we're afraid that it probably isn't. Nine times out of ten it all boils down to the same thing: Mum and Dad's relationship didn't work. Of course there'll be varying degrees of awfulness with regard to the level of lies, betrayal, hurt, unkindness and selfishness you suffered or inflicted, and how sad, upset, guilty and devastated you feel. To top it all, the timing could have been a real stinker. But in all cases you need to be able to move on from this horrible time so you can reach for the stars and grab your future. We want to help you find your way through this maze using our experiences and those of the hundreds of people we've met along our way. We've discovered from the single parents we've worked with that, no matter who did what to whom or whatever the ages of the children involved, the same issues come up time and time again and the same practical solutions can be applied to lots of situations.

Single-parent Families Can Be Great

Although it's by and large true that children from single-parent families are over-represented when it comes to low achievement, truancy, encounters with the law and other negative groups, we believe that it's not the fact that they're from single-parent families that causes the problems; it's what's going on in the family unit. Maybe it's because a single-parent family can be a stressful war zone, and that single parents on their own are too jiggered, unable or busy to provide adequate supervision and discipline.

Who knows? What we *do* know is that it doesn't have to be this way. It's totally within your power to create a new and fab family in which the children can thrive without the war and the stress, but with direction and energy.

Our Approach Is a Simple Version of a Traditional Family

We have a simple and effective approach, which is a re-interpretation of traditional family values – one that keeps both Mum and Dad in the picture (just separate frames! could even be different albums!), working together for the benefit of their children.

Our central philosophy is simple: you may no longer be together but you're still bonded forever through your children. Therefore it's in your best interests to crack on with developing a new working relationship with their dad. Treat him like a business partner and get on with it. Our key aim is to stop the war and win the peace, ensuring the children are never used as weapons or caught in any crossfire. We help people see that, no matter what has happened, there is a way out – and this is it!

The Rules, the Method and the Way to Succeed as a Single Parent

Here are the big ideas that are at the heart of our thinking and mean that your children can have a happy and stable childhood – while you get to have a life. Bravo! Hurrah!

They may be flipping obvious or appear hopelessly idealistic, and you may think 'Yeah, great in principle, but the stuff of daydreams' when you read them. But you may also get tingles of recognition or a sense of hope, or a feeling that we're talking about how you'd *like* things to be and that you too want a piece of the Kate and Emily action!

Stop the war and win the peace

No matter who did what to whom, it's in all of your interests to find a way of working through the aggro. There's too much at stake not to try to stop fighting. Peace (man) is good for you and the children.

Never use your child as a weapon

And never let them get caught in the crossfire. You may think you have justification – you don't. Fifty per cent of your child is your ex-partner – it's a biological fact. Don't mess with your child's self-esteem – it's just too dangerous an area to get into.

An ex is for life, not just for Christmas

You're still bonded together through your children, and you will be for the rest of their lives. You're not a single parent – you're a co-parent. Treat your ex like a business partner and *work* at it.

Look at it from your children's perspective

The No 1 most effective way to remain the adult when you're feeling irrational – and the easiest way to decide what's really the right thing to do – is to plant yourself in your children's shoes.

Do not confuse money with access

Controversial, but true: money and access are not related to each other – money will always mean power, so defuse the situation by becoming financially independent from each other as quickly as possible.

Remember, you still have a family

This is the one thing that hasn't changed, although the shape of it has. Your family still needs a leader, traditions, boundaries, fun and friends – just redrawn to fit a different frame.

Look after yourself and rebuild your future

Look after yourself, because you, your energy levels and happiness matter an awful lot to the success of your family. Life is for living and you have decades of fun ahead of you, so work positively towards a great future. If you don't throw a dart you won't hit the board, let alone the bullseye.

Be proud to do the right thing
One thing is guaranteed: the children will grow up and work it all out for themselves, and you want to be a hero. Creating a good example is also the easiest way to encourage 'others' to do the right thing.

Follow the rules – and do the work
Use the tools we give you in this book, from the personal MoT to the Code of Conduct, and stick to them for a whole year – no ifs, no buts. No matter what their dad does – you stay focused on what's best for you and the children and then tell us what we've said is a load of baloney!

How Did Kate Become a Single Parent?

Kate is an upbeat, laughing type – kind, though a bit on the feisty side. Reared in the south, her roots are northern. She calls a spade a spade. She has two children, a boy and a girl, rarely exercises (though always plans to), is keen on food, talking, laughing, *Coronation Street*, the library and holidays.

I am the third of four daughters born to a gentle southern doctor and a laughing midwife from the Lakes. We had an extremely happy childhood in the middle of the countryside. Having spent the first part of my education at a starchy all-girls school, I moved to the local mixed grammar school where I had enormous fun and managed somehow, despite the novelty of boys, to get decent enough A levels to get into university.

As soon as I left school I was like a rat out of a trap, guffawing around with friends throughout my twenties in flat-share land ... Men? They featured largely in films and romantic novels, always drop-dead handsome, masculine, strong, witty, 10-out-of-10 heroes and, to be frank, totally out of my league. The trouble was this made the idea of going out with a mere mortal who wore the wrong shoes, had light blue Y-fronts (I could see the waistband!) or drove a Sierra very unappealing. There were so many better things to do! Post graduation I made for the City and spent an extremely happy decade as a fund manager. I loved the buzz of the financial markets with access to all manner of interesting people and situations. I spent my days meeting the movers and groovers of UK industry, visiting companies, reading and trying to forecast the economy and yakking on the phone for hours, finding out what other people thought – and then, having come to my conclusions, ultimately dealing in shares to make the funds that I ran do well.

It's a miracle, when I look back, that I had any romantic adventures at all! I just loved laughing, eating, the cinema, the excitement of work and larking around with my friends. I skipped the normal steady boyfriend stuff – and for that lack of preparation I take some responsibility for the future breakdown of my marriage.

Anyhow, with my biological clock beginning to tick, I hooked up with, and wed, the chap who sat next to me at work. That really doesn't sound very romantic, does it? However he was (and is) a nice man and I thought he would make a good, steady partner. We had a marvellous wedding, moved into our house and started having babies. My daughter was born a year and a half later. While I was thrilled with my little girl, you'd have to have seen it to believe what happened to me: I fussed and worried all the time. She was so tiny and wouldn't eat, I felt she might break, and I couldn't bear to hear her cry. I spent my time at the biscuit barrel and only just managed to get out of maternity clothes. Housework was also not one of my areas of expertise. You can probably work out for yourself that I wasn't ticking many boxes as a housewife. So there was only one thing for it … back to work.

A degree of peace, harmony and order returned to our home for a while. However, I was so busy and tired, juggling a crying, non-eating baby, going to work and getting pregnant again that I didn't realize my husband had mentally checked out of our marriage.

By the time my son was born the wheels had well and truly come off my nuptials. My husband was a Peter Pan type, snared like a rabbit in the parent and thirty-something domestic scene. When he left, his cry was that there was no time for him and what he wanted to do. He'd found himself somewhere he didn't want to be. He was so convinced that there was no way back that he wasn't prepared to try. The children were three and one. I was 37 and had been married for five years. His leaving was a bolt from the blue. I literally had no idea that we were in trouble, and the degree of unhappiness he felt about his life with me came as a huge surprise. It took me a long time to adjust, accept and realize that I couldn't make it better.

Even though I can say all this quite rationally now, make no mistake: I can still get myself in a lather about the fact that my life and the children's lives have been determined by one person who (it seemed to me) cast us off, leaving me to cope. But with the help of friends and family I soon realized that the way forward was to do whatever I could to minimize the impact and distress that the children might feel. I also had a wake-up call when speaking to a very cross and bitter single mother at a party who, though technically beautiful, just seemed poisoned and ugly to me. I realized that I didn't want to be like her. I was also getting bored of seesawing between misery and anger. It made me feel bad, so I did that very hard thing of just 'letting it go'. Occupying my brain with lots of other people, activities and things, I forced myself not to obsess about my situation.

Being a good parent is important to me, as is giving my children a happy childhood, and although that plan had been knocked off course, I was (and still am) desperate to avoid unhappy offspring and want to give them a good grounding. I actively decided to help them develop a good relationship with their dad. Nothing I could do was going to change who he was, and the notion of using the children to punish him seemed short-sighted, stupid, barking mad, ridiculous and cruel.

Interestingly, I soon found that the nicer and more reasonable I was to my ex-husband, the more I got out of the deal. Whenever I upped the ante or behaved in a negative or confrontational way (even if this was the result of tiredness or exasperation) I usually got a negative response, which was counter-productive and always a step backwards, and left me feeling horrible. I initiated divorce proceedings, lost tonnes of weight, got a new job and, with a new attitude on my shoulders, started having fun. I met a new man, fell madly in love and had a couple of years of romance. However, the children's needs, my fussy parenting style, a chaotic life and the demands of a childless man turned out to be incompatible and more than I could juggle.

The children are now both at school. We're a very happy and close little unit of three, with a large extended family and some brilliant friends. The children love their father dearly, see him regularly and believe with true conviction that he's the greatest dad on the planet – and in lots of ways he is.

Every now and then I still struggle with the issues created by my situation. I sometimes feel alone, weighed down by responsibility, unable to plan for the future, fed up with being broke, sorry for myself, tired, disappointed for the children and hugely sad about what has happened. However, I do have a naturally upbeat personality, and pretty much every day there's something that makes me laugh LOUD. I've a great sense of delight that I've so much to be grateful for – most importantly, of course, my two wonderful children. To be honest, when I'm feeling sad that I didn't have more children and am not enjoying the comfortable family life I thought I'd have, I nearly always stop myself and think 'Thank goodness I've these two gems.' I wouldn't swap them for anything. They make it impossible to regret any of it. And to be totally honest, however indignant I may feel I can also recognize that I married the wrong man, for which I must take responsibility. The future I'd imagined and thought had been stolen from me was a fantasy of my own making.

How Did Emily Become a Single Parent?

Emily is a jolly, laid-back, grounded sort. She has two children, a boy and a girl, and is keen on *The Archers*, wine, laughing, company, parties and loud bars, listening to the radio, lavatorial jokes, birds, bees and pets. This is the story of how she became a single parent.

I'm a South Londoner born and bred, with a younger brother. My family was (and still is) very close; when I was growing up, home was a very nice place to be (bar the odd teenage spat I threw my parents' way!). My schooling was, to coin a phrase, 'a game of two halves'. In one half I was toughened up at a mixed south London primary school, and in the other half I was softened up at an all-girls secondary school. The summer I left school was two months of growing up and discovering the fun of leaving home.

It was the 1980s and I embraced the work hard/play hard culture (did I say 'work hard'? That was an error!). I've lasting memories of lunch hours spent in the pub with 'Sales', of Amanda's, James', Johnnies (in the nice sense!), white wine spritzers and dancing 1980s style into the small hours (as my friend Wedgie always said, 'When you're out, you're out!'). Then there was Oxford Poly, with shared houses, leaving dirty dishes for days on end, bikes, toast with chocolate powder on, diet milkshakes, books sitting untouched whilst talking endlessly about nothing meaningful in the coffee lounge and making some very good friends. I travelled for a year with my best friend Lizzy, working as we went to raise money to finance the next leg of our travels. It was a huge adventure, a big melting pot of people and friendships – and memories that are still very fresh after 20 years!

I returned from my travels still with wanderlust in my rucksack and very little enthusiasm for the real world. A lovely neighbour, who's more of a surrogate big sister, gave me the lecture that I certainly wouldn't take from my mum or dad: she told me to get a grip of my knickers and get a job. So my career in market research started, and continues to this day.

I was sharing a house with a bunch of mates in London when I met my husband-to-be at a friend's 24th birthday party. We married two years later when we were both 26. After four years together we started a family and had two children, a girl and a boy with 18 months between them. The children were (and are!) wonderful, but hard work. The first few years were spent in a flurry of nappies, baby wipes, colic, giggles and tantrums – every parent knows the sort of thing.

Who knows what happened? Perhaps we divided and conquered a bit too much and began to think of ourselves as individuals rather than a couple. Or perhaps we were too complacent about our relationship and just assumed that we'd always be together, so we didn't pay our marriage much attention. Anyway, the end result was that, as the children grew older and I could lift my head up and peer over the pile of nappies, I realized that I was unhappy. It seemed that we had both changed a little as we'd got older and had slowly grown apart. I could no longer contain my unhappiness so that it didn't affect my children or husband. I told my husband how I felt and asked him to leave. This is a very blunt way of putting it, but I suppose it's what I did. It was the hardest and most horrible thing I have ever done, and ever expect to do. If I could have, I would have asked him to stay, but I couldn't. I was (and thankfully still am) convinced that every member of the family would be happier if we separated than if we stayed together.

I felt guilty, and that guilt made me want to make things as painless as possible. I had an overwhelming desire to be fair and accommo-dating, and also a need to balance being a mother with working towards total financial independence. I was as flexible as I could be about all of the divorce and access arrangements. I didn't feel that I had any right to complain about feeling dejected, overworked, tired, etc. It's hard to kick the thought that says 'You broke it up, you take the consequences.' So it's hard to accept help, or even admit you need it. As to the future, it took several years and my ex-husband moving on by getting remarried before the feeling of being in limbo went. Up until then I was waiting to see what he did with his life so that I could see what I could do with mine. I didn't feel I had the right to be the one to drive on first. But now I have the feeling that my life is my own to determine, I just need to grab it!

I might have been the one to end my marriage, but I'm not totally different from single parents who have been left. I too have money worries and can feel overcome by the feeling of responsibility. I can reach my wits' end dealing with the children, house and work. I can feel full of self-pity and loneliness, and dream of having someone who cares about me as much as I care about them. I daydream of stopping: stopping having to do anything, getting off the merry-go-round for a bit. My idea of a holiday and a rest is not having to make one single decision. One day I'd love to get off the merry-go-round by beekeeping and having a vegetable patch. I'll listen to *The Archers* and *I'm Sorry I Haven't a Clue*. I'll sit at a desk with just enough work to do that fills a day rather than eats into nights and weekends. I'll be staring out of the window watching the grey tits nest in my window box. I'll continue to be entertained by my mis-chievous children and have a large, warm kitchen and hearth. And, in between times, I'll follow Stephen Fry, Paul Merton and Billy

Connolly around. Or perhaps they'll pop round one evening to join me and a few friends in a glass of wine or two.

Why Kate Thought the World Needed a Fresh Approach to Single Parenting

I met Emily when we were both married, at a babies music class when our oldest two were toddlers. We've been friends ever since. We found ourselves in the single-parent boat together, offering each other a marvellous source of support, tonic and amusement. I thought we'd be a good team: Emily is more thoughtful, where I shoot from the hip; I talk, she listens; I let it all out and she keeps it all in. She understands teaching, coaching and human behaviour, and I do practical money and things. I thought that we should do something together. I had a dream, a plan, an idea born out of my experience as a single mum. You see, finding other single mums and making friends with at least one of them can be great. The benefits of not having to explain, being able to laugh and not feeling so different are enormous. As I didn't know any other single parents, I had to be quite proactive in finding some. So, creating a mechanism for single parents to find each other locally (just as antenatal groups do at a different turning point) became one of my motivations for starting 'Kate and Emily'.

My other motivation wasn't social; it was more to do with finding out what other people like me were doing and how they were managing. Just as I spent ages discussing different ways of feeding and entertaining little ones with other new mums, I wanted to find out what other single mums did to cope – did they let their children sleep in their bed? Did they let their ex-husband have a set of house keys? How were they explaining things to their children? So 'Kate and Emily' needed to be a support *and* social network.

When I broached the idea to Emily, luckily for me she'd had a particularly crap day at work and so said 'Yes!' Although not entirely sure what she was saying 'Yes' to, she went into clipboard mode. The next thing I knew we were brainstorming, buying domain names and running focus groups, finding out exactly how single mums felt and what they wanted. The starting gun had sounded ... we were off. It had to be the best perk of being single that we could decide to do madcap things like 'Kate and Emily'.

That was 2003 and we haven't looked back. We set up a local club for single parents and have listened and learned as loads of single mums have discussed in groups, participated in workshops, had fun together and chewed the cud concerning all facets of being a single parent.

We made a 15-part television series for Discovery Home and Health called *Single Mums SOS*. Our website (www.kateandemily.com) is vibrant, quirky and no-nonsense, with an active agony section and practical tools to help single parents move on, do the best for their children, and get along well enough with each other to parent effectively, and so 'Kate and Emily' has expanded from a local group to a national resource.

There's a commonly held misconception that people's situations are so different that it would be impossible to write a book to suit everyone. However, we've discovered that whoever did what to whom, whatever the ages of the children or the period of time that has elapsed since the separation, the same six or seven issues come up time and time again. We've also found that the same practical solutions can be applied to the variations on a theme – not necessarily always to the letter, but certainly in spirit. We don't muddy the waters by focusing on extreme and unusually awful situations, and although we know that your journey will surely have been difficult, to keep harping back on the negative side might make you feel worse rather than better. So brace yourself for an upbeat book!

Let this Book Help You Make Life Better for You and Yours

We know this isn't a book you wanted to buy or to be given. We know this isn't an aspirational book to have on the coffee table. So we've made it as easy and as palatable to work through as possible.

We want you to get ideas from this book, and from those ideas to create solutions that'll work for you and your situation. Having done this you can devise your own plan and stick to it. Think of the money paid for this book as an investment!

If you're into browsing, then focus on our top tips and bullet points. If you're struggling to see how to put it into practice, read the 'Dear Kate and Emily' bits. These 'Dear Kate and Emily's are based on letters sent to us and people's descriptions of real problems. You might recognise the conundrum and the situation being described, but we've changed key bits of information to keep them anonymous hence the witty names. If you identify with the situation or issues they're addressing then our answer will mean something to you and give you some ideas on how to improve things in your own life.

We believe that we've the best qualifications in the world to write this book, though sadly none is recognized by any professional body or association! We're qualified because we live it and because we've talked to more single mums than you could shake a stick at. We know the subjects that you might want to think about, and where it'd be worth your while to take some time out to ponder a little longer. This is where we've gone for audience participation and come up with some worksheets and questions for you to think about and answer. They're supposed to be like full stops – making you take a natural pause before galloping on! Remember, things are not black and white. Even if you don't write your answers in this book or anywhere else, do shut your eyes and think about the questions, and try to think honestly and self-critically. Make a note (actual or mental) of what you think might work for you.

If you get bogged down thinking 'This is never going to work,' take a break and come back to it. Keep pressing on and gathering what you can.

Chapter 2

LEAVING THE PAST BEHIND AND GETTING INTO THE GROOVE

People become single parents for loads of different reasons, some more messy than others. Whatever happened, you must look to the future and leave the past behind. You need to find a way to work through the ins and outs of your failed relationship so that you can park that piece of history. The motivation? There's a lot of unscripted life in front of you yet!

If we had a pound for every time someone asked us how long it'd be until they felt better, we'd be swimming in the filthy stuff (or at least nearly enough for a night out). Our stock answer is always 'Two years,' so if you've done six months, you've got about 547 days left. This is what a rather anal analytical (male!) friend told Kate when she was moaning on, and Kate, being a facts-and-figures type of person, appreciated knowing that she wasn't looking at infinity. Oddly enough, he was right. It seems that although there will be ups and downs, and certainly an improving trend, it seems to generally come out as a couple of years.

How you feel after your split and how you come to terms with the situation will probably go through four distinct phases, which we've discovered is a process well documented and as old as the hills. Here's that process so you can see where you are and what's to come.

What Steps to Expect along the Journey

Step 1 – Denial

Denial is a totally natural reaction to a shock or surprise. This may be how you felt when you discovered that your partnership was in major trouble. *How can this be? I had no idea. I thought we were so happy. Yes, we had ups and downs, but doesn't everyone? This can't be happening!*

As a result of an inability to deal with the reality of the situation, you might find yourself suggesting all sorts of things that would've been unthinkable in the past, just to make the problems go away and turn back the clock. We're thinking of things such as sanctioning infidelity, offering to give up work, to lose five stone, to never see your parents again, to turn into someone else, etc. Denial's also about believing that the man who has told you clearly and repeatedly that he no longer wants to live with you, and goes off to live in Alaska with Sven following a civil partnership ceremony at Marylebone registry office, is just having a 'funny turn' and will come back home and everything will be as it always was, with you both spending Sunday afternoons sitting in deckchairs watching Sven do the gardening in his Speedos.

When you come to the point of compromising yourself completely, and dropping your moral standards, or when you know that you've NO respect left for your partner and you STILL think it'll be all right, STOP! You're in denial: get with the programme, it is over.

People who do the leaving can also be in denial, usually assuming that everything will be better once they've separated and that they and their ex-husband will remain good friends after the divorce. Emily believes that when you're thinking about ending your marriage you're doing it in a relatively detached and calm way as you decide what's the best thing for you and your family. If you decide the best thing is for the marriage to end, then you can't help but hope that everyone else will see it this way. If only that were true ... So there's a nice way of getting divorced, then? No! You'll all be good friends, then? Definitely not at the outset – and while it's anyone's guess about the future, it is without doubt tricky.

Either way, dumper or dumpee, one day it'll dawn on you that this is for real and that it isn't the set of a very bad film you've stumbled onto, nor is it your trashy holiday read or something that happens to other people. This is your life and you've got to deal with it.

Dear Kate and Emily,
My husband and I have been together since we were teenagers. We're best friends and love each other dearly. We've been bliss-fully happy for 11 years, we rarely argue and we understand each other totally. I've always been his little treacle pudding and I couldn't want for more. So imagine my surprise when I came back from a weekend away with the girls to find he'd packed his bags and moved in with someone else. He says he's gone for good to follow his dreams. I don't understand it at all, he hardly knows this woman, she got her claws into him at a point in his life when he was vulnerable. That was three years ago and I just want my husband back now. He has good contact with the children, so I do see him. When he comes to the house it's as though he's been taken over by an alien force, he's there in body but not in spirit. I am sure that we can forget about all this, I've lost two stone and would do anything to turn the clock back. Does any of this make sense to you?
Love,
In Denial from Derby

Dear In Denial,

We hate to be harsh, but we've got to come clean and say that none of it does make sense to us. We all hope for things: that our children will grow up fit and happy, that it won't rain during a picnic, that England will win the World Cup, that last year's summer clothes will still fit, that we'll find a fabulous love match. There's nothing wrong with hope, and we know life becomes impossible when we've given it all up. But there comes a time when we have to let go of one of the things we hope for — like a husband returning back home after three years as if nothing has happened.

Drop that particular hope, but keep the others that are tied up with it — like 'I hope to be happy again,' 'I hope to be someone's treacle pudding again' and 'I hope to be loved again.' All those hopes and dreams are still possible — just not with that particular man. So look for them with someone else. The sooner you accept it, the sooner you'll be able to give yourself a chance to mourn your loss and then dust yourself down and look forward to the next love.

Love, Kate and Emily

Step 2 – Grief

Grief is when the reality of your situation slaps you in the face, when you've tried everything you can to make things better and it still hasn't worked and now the pain sets in. You might feel depressed and tearful and bogged down by your own situation and believe that you'll never find anyone or that no one else will ever want you. This is the stage where you could be in danger of going round and round in circles as you make your friends relive the whole affair and indulge in lots of post-match analysis. Make no mistake, this is real grief: the family and life you'd planned are over and nothing now is going to be the way you'd imagined. Future children you wanted and planned in your head may not be born, no silver wedding celebrations, no more 'my husband and I'. Or at least for now it seems like this. Your world and the future you forecast has ended and you really can't yet imagine a new one.

Grief can sap you of confidence as you focus on the negatives, failure and what you feel you've lost. It's frightening and really makes you realize how much has changed about your life. These losses will almost certainly have made you feel some of the emotions listed on the right-hand side of our list:

You May have Lost	You May Feel
Future children	Bereft
Money	Jealous of other people
Home	Envy
Possessions	Green-eyed monsterish
Job	Failure
Family and friends	Sad
Dreams	Without a future
Ambitions	Angry
Freedom and choice	It's so unfair
Status	Failure
Identity	Embarrassed
Hope	Defeated
Shared parenting	I didn't want this for them
Husband	Lonely
Protection	Frightened

Your future has been knocked off course and this grief needs to be recognized and accepted. Getting through to 'acceptance' can be pretty painful and messy. So make the most of the time you're on your own – when the children are at school, in bed or out – and think about working through this very difficult phase. Here are some top tips from people who've walked this path before you:

- 'Scream and shout if you feel like it or go to bed and wrap your duvet around you. Though do limit the time you let yourself wallow alone feeling sad and crying.'
- 'Keep your strength up and accept as much help as you're offered. If a neighbour offers to do a school run, say "Yes." If someone offers to babysit – take it.'
- 'Let your friends know you're raw and need a bit of TLC.'
- 'Look after yourself just as you would if you were on a sicky. You know the sort of thing: lots of bed, watching brainless TV, let the housework slip and if you don't want to go out, don't ...'
- 'Sleep. And if you find it impossible, see your doctor.'
- 'If alternative therapies are your thing, now is the time for a relaxing treatment or at least a lavender bath!'
- 'Invite a friend or relative to stay, or make sure you get away at the weekends.'

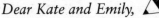

Dear Kate and Emily,
My husband has left me and our two girls to go and live with his secretary. I feel as though I can't cope. Quite simply my heart is broken and I don't know what to do. I only ever wanted to be a wife and a mother, a homemaker, to welcome him home after a hard day at the office – he was our hero and I feel as though I've wasted my life on him. I can't bear this, I feel so full of uncontrollable emotions. I hate him, scream at him, fight with him and his new girlfriend. They've destroyed my family. I cry and cry and can't stop. The children know he's broken my heart. They care so much for me and try to comfort me; I don't know what I'd have done without them. I want to be happy,

but it feels as though there's no light at the end of the tunnel.
Love,
Broken-hearted of Bromley

Dear Broken-hearted,

You're in a shocking place at the moment; it must all seem so dark and hard to deal with. The children are a great strength, aren't they? Sometimes it's simply knowing that you've got to get them up, dressed, fed and entertained that keeps you going through these very horrible times. But we're afraid that's where the help the children can give you must end. They must be allowed to have only childish, rather than adult, worries on their shoulders. So use their presence and their need to be mothered to keep you going and to provide structure, but do deal with your own very painful journey away from them as much as you can. If you need someone to talk to maybe it's worth a trip to the GP, who can recommend a counsellor. If you're a churchgoer someone there may be able to help, or even a close and trusted family member. But at the end of the day this is not about getting answers or solutions, it's about you processing the information in a way that helps you to understand and move on.

Another idea is to write letters to your ex, his girlfriend, the children, anyone you want to. Put them in an envelope and seal it — but DON'T SEND IT! Write whatever you want, just make sure it's for your eyes only.

Even if you've never done such a thing, buy a page-a-day diary and get into the habit of spending 10 minutes a day spilling out your thoughts. Why not start each day's entry with the three best things that happened that day? The journal will soon serve marvellously to demonstrate why you're so glad to be you! Then just let rip — Yes — write the bad stuff down, and every once in a while allow yourself to reflect on the really difficult things that have happened (we call it 'delving around in your bottom drawer'!).

You'll not believe how far and fast you can come. If the same things seem to be upsetting you for an abnormally long length of time, then they need to be pulled out, disentangled and dealt with. Don't edit yourself; just write. You'll find that as you do your mind will process it all in a different way, and if you're lucky you'll get to a point where it all falls into place, your cloud will lift and your brain will be saying to you — 'It's OK, park it, c'est l'histoire!' Then burn it and tell yourself that it's time to get a smile back on your face and a bit of a wiggle on!

Love, Kate and Emily

Thankfully we all know that even though this is an important phase, it can't last for ever. What tends to happen is that you'll find you won't be able to bear it after a while and you'll become tired of feeling flat and full of self-pity and introspection. Your nearest and dearest will want you to get back to your old self and will be bored of you raking over the coals. Bang on about the break-up for too long and you'll find that they'll be practically unable to talk to you about anything else, and that doesn't help anyone. You may also realize that your mood is affecting your children (however brave in front of them you are, they have excellent antennae), and this is usually a very good jolt back to planet 'enough-is-enough'!

The consequences of living with many of the negative emotions associated with this stage are debilitating. Eventually you'll feel poisoned and want it to stop. To stop it you'll need to find short-term ways of managing these feelings as you come to accept your situation and then work towards the future.

So we move into Emily's 'get a grip' department. It's now time to:

- Stop talking about it. Tell your friends you're going to take a break from talking about it, and steer discussions more towards planning activity-based nights out, gossiping about other people, and documentaries and period dramas on the telly.

- Get out of the house. Kate recommends a trip to the library to see what's going on locally; Emily suggests making for somewhere packed with people for a bit of a buzz and lifting of the spirits (even a packed commuter train can feel rather comforting!).
- Force yourself to see the glass as half-full rather than half-empty, and go about ordering a top-up.
- Try to stop thinking about it and divert your brain by keeping yourself busy.
- Get on the phone and talk to mates and fill up your diary.
- Start smiling and saying hello – and don't tell every Tom, Dick and Harry how you really feel, just say 'Fine, thanks' and change the subject.

Step 3 – Anger

Now you've done denial and grief, it's time for 'furious', where dreams of revenge are sweet and sadistic. Negative emotions such as anger, hurt and revenge can be so powerful they can make us all behave like completely irrational fruit bats. We can't make these feelings disappear, but we do suggest that dealing with them *away* from the children and beginning to understand your past and reconciling yourself to your future are key to moving onwards and upwards.

As anger is a powerful emotion, the best plan for moving away from it is to cut off its oxygen supply. Here's how:

- Don't rise to the bait.
- Don't argue back.
- Know that you're doing the right thing.
- Don't discuss the contents of your 'bottom drawer'.
- Don't badmouth, rise above it.
- Don't let other people fan the flames.

- Remember, bad words are addictive – let one out and more will follow.
- Look to the future.

If you find that you've gone a bit passive, it could be that you're storing your fury up – that way lies a future explosion! The received wisdom is that if you skip one of these four phases you're less likely to mend your broken heart, so if you try to blow past this one, or bury it, you're likely to find yourself taking your anger (or your grief) out on the wrong person. If anger is a stage you just can't get into, then the top tip is to brainstorm all the things that you might be angry about. Pen, paper, your drink of choice, an uninterrupted couple of hours and a box of tissues and you're bound to come up with a list! Then get physical about it, because anger needs activity: scrub the house, dig the garden, go for a brisk walk, run, put the music on and disco dance.

You'll know an old heartbreak is affecting a new relationship if you over-react to something your new partner does that reminds you of your old one: for example, walking out of the pub in disgust because he smacks his lips and says 'Ahhhh' after the first gulp of a pint, just like your ex used to, might be a sign of such an over-reaction!

Step 4 – Acceptance

There'll come a stage when you'll be able to talk about your ex-husband, or hear news of him, without spiralling into decline. You'll feel more detached as he takes a place in your romantic past. There's a pithy little phrase, 'This too will pass' – and it's true, it does, because that's the way we're made – thank goodness!

However, be warned, getting here can take years. You mustn't be hard on yourself about it. You may still feel sad and fed up, but it'll be like bereavement: the intensity of how you feel will come and go in waves, but you'll be able to deal with it and incorporate it into the rich tapestry of your life. If you're finding you can't, then you need to see the doc and talk about it.

Many of us carry the baggage of old break-ups around, and this can mess with our minds. It seems that the more break-ups we go through, the more our mental health's affected. This suggests that we're not getting over them. We have to go through the natural process of loss and mourning. There's no way round it. The experts tell us that, generally, we'd most of us rather skirt round painful stuff than tackle it head-on, because skirting always looks shorter and easier. Wrong! It's like going around a bramble patch and finding you fall off a precipice instead! So, when the ghost of an old relationship pops up to threaten a new one, ask yourself: 'Is this really about now, or is it about then?' The answer might be both, but asking yourself helps to keep those ghosts in check.

It's been one huge learning curve and a wonderful, tearful, fulfilling, soul-destroying, happy, educational, frustrating and fun-filled journey. I can't honestly say that I wouldn't have missed it for the world, but I can't turn the clock back and it has ultimately made me into the woman I am today. I'll never know the woman I might have been, had I remained with my husband, but I know that today I am a confident, happy, career-doing-well 49-year-old mother of two energetic teenage boys. The whole single-parent journey has proved that I'm a survivor. The turning point that proved this to me came shortly after the birth of my second son. I was sitting on the floor in a corner of my bedroom sobbing my heart out and feeling sorry for myself, when something told me that I had a choice – I could curl up in a corner and give up, or I could get up, dry my eyes and embrace life and whatever it throws at me. Fortunately for all concerned, I got up and dried my eyes!
A Single Mum

Maybe You Don't Recognize these Steps?

Maybe you've done the dumping and these four steps don't ring any bells with you? Emily clearly recalls how she didn't seem to be feeling the same as the other single mums were. Instead of this journey, you might be feeling all sorts of other emotions, like a feeling of relief, guilt, concern, a sense of overwhelming responsibility and pressure not to let the wheels come off your cart. Emily felt apart from others because she couldn't be angry or feel grief. She felt heartless and cold because she just seemed to accept it and get on with it. This is what she says about it all:

> When I first came across these four steps I felt a total fraud, as I couldn't really recognize them. I felt horrible for putting my ex-husband through them and heartless for just feeling 'acceptance'. So I dug around in my 'bottom drawer' to remind myself of the journey I'd gone through to get from married to separated. I made myself remember the whole process from beginning to end. Looking back I could remember clearly feeling physically sick, more alone than ever before and incredibly miserable and guilty. Recalling these horrible times was strangely useful and has made me feel as normal, human and complex as everyone else. It's odd I had to work back from 'acceptance' to spot the other three steps before I could well and truly park my history.

Let's Think Honestly about the Failed Relationship

It's not just these four steps that help you to 'park your history'; it's also having a very honest review of your old relationship and coming to see how both you and your ex must take some responsibility for it ending. This is what the next section's about.

You have to stand back and be very honest when you read this section, as there's rather a lot of soul-searching to do! We really don't believe that it's possible to have a good relationship with someone who doesn't want one with you. Nor do we believe that loving, contented partners can be stolen away from each other against their will. A good relationship surely needs TWO people who are dedicated to each other and to the relationship. The stereotypes of single mothers as victims to be pitied, or selfish people who didn't try hard enough, aren't accurate. In reality, single mothers are simply people whose relationship didn't work. When it comes to accepting history and moving on, it's worth acknowledging that you may be a bit lost and are resisting the reality of your situation. Could it be you're rewriting history to suit the situation you find yourself in and the way you want to be perceived?

Were Red Flags Flying?

Looking back honestly, were there warning signs that your relationship was in choppy waters? In this section we want you to really start thinking about your past relationship objectively. How it *really* was (rather than how it was at its best, or how it seemed to the outside world, or how you imagined it was). Nobody's watching or listening except for you, so try to be honest with yourself, as there's a very good chance that this will help you move on. Was your relationship littered with red flags flying that you chose to ignore? We're thinking red flags like: was sex really a bit rubbish? did he really feel like a kindred spirit? In all probability you and your husband share the blame for your relationship failing, and if you call on a 'no-holds-barred' hindsight, you may be able to identify the moment when your first red flag appeared and you questioned your relationship. If you're really honest, did these red flags keep on flying?

So go on, get paper, pen, thinking cap, bev of choice and list the red flags that were telling you your relationship wasn't the stuff of Mills and Boon. Let's start at the very beginning.

Just about everyone has a red flag or eight – here are some from people we've spoken to:

- 'I can remember how devastatingly disappointing the first kiss was.'

- 'I found myself looking at him through other people's eyes and feeling embarrassed about what I saw!'
- 'He forgot my birthday and I realized I wasn't top of his list anymore.'
- 'My male friends clearly were not that impressed and didn't seem to want to bond with him, which felt odd.'
- 'On my wedding day he asked me to lie about my dad's job on our marriage certificate. I went cold.'
- 'Some while into our relationship but before our marriage, he told me about his early sexual exploits, which I found a bit creepy. My hero wouldn't have done that!'
- 'When my gran died and I didn't need him.'
- 'When, having had sex, I'd breathe a sigh of relief and think, 'That's that box ticked for a week!''
- 'When I thought about things that I wanted to do, rather than about things for us as a couple to do.'
- 'When I got back from a girls weekend and couldn't wait to see the children and he didn't cross my mind.'
- 'When the thought of spending the weekend just *en famille* without seeing anyone else felt like a desperate option to be avoided at all costs.'
- 'When he turned up to meet me from work in an orange anorak, indecent running shorts, sandals and socks with Road Runner cartoons on!'
- 'Reading about a car crash in the paper and it dawning on me that actually a car crash might make sorting out the marriage easier.'
- 'When I heard other people complaining about their husbands' golfing and I realized that I just wouldn't have cared less whether he golfed every Saturday or not.'
- 'Realizing one day that we hadn't had sex for six months and didn't really mind.'

Almost everyone who has ever split up will have some of these types of memories. If you've got to the point of separation still believing that you had a happy, successful marriage, you're likely to be deluding yourself. We don't say that to be horrible, but to make you think more honestly about the situation so that you can realize, acknowledge and accept that you did have something to do with the failure. The whole point of which is that it makes dealing with Dad for the sake of the children a whole lot easier, and helps you to move on feeling less of a victim or the bad guy.

A Huge Turning Point

Realizing that the relationship wasn't great for either of you is a huge turning point because it means you can focus on dealing with the fall-out – the hurt and humiliation, the blow to your pride and self-esteem – much better. Coping with these is a much more manageable task once you can get to the stage where you can write a full and frank paragraph which starts, 'My marriage failed because ...' and then describes the *real* reasons for your marriage's failure. Most importantly, you'll be able to do this with a degree of balance when apportioning blame. Even if you feel totally badly done by, you might need to go back further and think about whether you married the wrong man, made the wrong choice, wanted children more than you wanted a husband, preferred being with your friends, were sexually incompatible, didn't keep trying, ignored niggles that all was not well, and so on.

Having Digested Your Break-up, It's Much Easier to Look to the Future

After you've put the break-up into perspective and you understand it as much as it's possible to, and once you've grieved and thrown tubs of ice-cream in anger, it's now time to focus on the opportunities that might lie ahead. When you were part of a couple you had to take your husband into consideration, his opinions and views. You'll have compromised on many things. But now, if you want to watch *Corrie* at full volume munching your way through a bag of cheese and onion, you can. No more wrestling with the radio dial whizzing between *The Archers Omnibus* and 5 Live!

If you want to plan a weekend walking, do it. Try and look back to things that were a part of your life in the past; whether it's music you no longer listen to, knitting, matchstick models or crafts, theatre or squash. Try and remember how you used to enjoy yourself and see if you can kick-start an old habit (legal and age-appropriate!).

Alternatively, consider things or hobbies you've always wanted to pursue, and set yourself some deadlines to start doing them. If you repeatedly think about starting things and never get round to them, then consider telling someone else your plans. Going public and promising action's a damn fine way of getting off your bottom and doing it!

Here we've pooled together things that other people have told us they did when they, too, needed to rediscover life on their own:

- 'When my ex left I decorated my bedroom and changed all the furniture so I didn't have to sleep in 'our' bedroom any more.'
- 'When I was younger I was a big reader, but I got out of the habit as my husband wasn't a book lover. I never got to go and buy books, so I took that up again and would lose myself in a story for a while. I love hanging around bookshops; some even have built-in coffee shops.'
- 'One word … YOGA.'
- 'I say 'yes' to as much as I can.'
- 'I'm going to do a pottery course. It's free and they have a crèche.'
- 'I make sure that I go out with the girls for a night out about once every 6–8 weeks.'
- 'Jumping and dancing around and singing at the top of my voice has to be one of the best therapies for me. (It also helps that the children love the same music as me, so we all lose it together!)'
- 'The Scissor Sisters and Meatloaf played very, very loud.'
- 'I get out to a college class one night a week. I decided to try and focus my nights out away from food and drink, so I picked something I'd never have thought of doing. Not really a hobby but it does give me a legitimate reason to be out. I did Web

Design last year and even got a certificate!'
- 'I love online jigsaws when I get time. I've come to value my own company, which I never did before.'
- 'I started belly dancing three weeks ago, and it's FAB as it's something completely frivolous and daft, and *just for me*!'
- 'I garden. I've got an allotment. Spending 2–3 hours a day there saves me from insanity.'
- 'I love colouring in (there's nothing like sharpening the lead in your pencil, as the actress said to the bishop). (*Pathetic, Emily! – Kate*)'

    After my first marriage I've experienced such a period where
I had the feeling that everything was going wrong, where I was
angry at everyone, but that also gave me the power to fight.
JK Rowling, *The Daily Mail* 5th December 2007

    You look back at the good bits and the bad bits, and you think,
were the good bits that good? You churn the whole thing over
and, oh, it's exhausting trying to make sense of something that in
the end you can't make sense of. But it shakes your perception of
yourself on a really basic level. You think of yourself as a part of a
couple and then you're not. It takes getting used to. *[Therapy
helped Victoria to deal with the upset and she was assured her grief
was perfectly normal.]* Normally it's irritating not to be unique but
in this case it was a huge comfort to me.
Victoria Wood. (Copyright © *Victoria Wood: The Biography*,
Neil Brandwood 2006, Virgin Books Ltd.)

Chapter 3

LOOKING AFTER YOU

It's not by chance that a chapter all about looking after yourself has found its way towards the beginning of this book. Kate's mother has often reminded her, 'If you don't put yourself at the top of the pile, no one else will.' Mind you, to be honest, Kate doesn't need much reminding!

However, as we've gone about our business we've come across many a single mum who feels that looking after herself is just one of those things that has to give. These mums know, and accept, that they're neglecting themselves, but this realization is usually swiftly followed by 'Well, I don't have time, money or energy for me anyway,' plus a whole raft of other reasons used to justify why they think they're not 'worth it'. As if spending time on themselves is tantamount to skiving off! Nothing could be further from the truth.

Whatever's going on in your life, ignoring your own needs is *not* a good move. We don't see 'me time' as a skive, nor as self-indulgent, nor as effort and energy that could've been better spent on the children. It's vital, and to everyone's benefit. IS THAT CLEAR?!

Sometimes it might seem as though you want to let the world

know how rubbish it all is by letting yourself go around looking like a bag of old spanners, or by not bothering to think about the future, or wallowing in your misery. It's a sort of 'Look what a terrible time I'm having' type of behaviour. Try to knock that on the head, and remember that when it comes to taking care of yourself, you're your own greatest resource and worst enemy!

Time Audit

Writing things down can make you realize what you're really spending most of your time doing, and can show you that by cutting a few corners (like not ironing sheets!) you could actually gain a bit more time for yourself.

It may seem a bit of a drag, but go on a fact-finding mission to see where your time is going. If you complete the following 'time audit' for three to seven days you'll soon see a pattern developing (try and do at least one of each different 'type of day' – e.g. a weekday and a Saturday or Sunday, a work day and a non-work day, a child-free day and a with-child day). The idea of the audit's to find out how much time you spend on various activities across the day. Activities are at the top of the audit chart, and down the side is the 24-hour clock in 30-minute slots. For each slot, record what you spent the majority of that half-hour doing. Once you've filled in the time audit for several days, add up the total number of hours spent on each activity and ask yourself:

- Does it look healthy? (Am I sleeping enough? Am I on my own too much?)
- Am I wasting time? Could some of it be better spent?
- Where can I make more time for me? Or use the time I've got free more constructively?

	Sleep	Me-time/Relaxing	Out and about	Chatting on the phone	Looking after the children	Fun with the children	Housework	Cooking	Errands/Shopping	Working
5.30										
6.00										
6.30										
7.00										
etc										

Reality Check

When we say look after yourself, we don't mean abandon camp for a holiday in Tenerife with no more than a couple of ready meals and a 14-year-old babysitter for the children. But we *do* want you to remember that you're an individual, separate from the children. We'd go so far as to berate those who are not taking adequate care of themselves, and may even say that you're not doing your best for your children, the atmosphere in your home or the happiness of your family. We say these harsh and firm phrases to make you realize that how you're coping is an important cornerstone to your success as a single parent.

The way you're coping with your situation, now and in the future, will have an impact on your stress levels, which has such a huge bearing on the children and their behaviour.

The very real and positive benefits which will result from a bit of self-nurturing include:

- greater energy levels – which will give you more power to do everything that's asked of you
- a better vibe in your home
- increasing the rate at which you're able to move on
- encouraging your children to value 'you'; this is a great lesson to teach children
- feeling more relaxed with your children's dad
- your children feeling able to enjoy their dad knowing that you're happy
- making you happier and more fulfilled, and less fearful of the future.

And finally, being really harsh:

- It'll make you more appealing to be around, not only for friends (old and new), but if a new partner is what you're after, then it's vital ... don't you think? Who wants to be around a doormat who doesn't value herself? Someone who wants to take advantage, we reckon – so drop the doormat line and start to look after yourself.

It's Not Always Easy

We do know that for some it's very, very hard to put yourself at the top of the pile. Often this is because not only do you have to look after children, home, money, in fact everything, by yourself now, but on top of all that you may feel a bit trampled as a result of having to ...

- try to find the resources to be a strong, consistent and good parent when you're at the end of your tether
- give your children a great, carefree, happy childhood in the midst of your own adult problems

- be fair with your children when your own situation doesn't feel fair
- work with someone with whom you now have a broken relationship.

Acknowledge that a lot is demanded of you, just so you can appreciate that you really MUST make sure you're OK and give yourself a fighting chance. At the very least, try always to have a good night's sleep!

If you're still finding it hard to move on, then be warned – most of us get pretty fed up of being fed up and thinking miserable stuff, and want to get a grip eventually. We reckon it takes between 12 and 18 months, and surely no more than two years, to stop feeling really deeply unhappy. If you're still in the depths of misery and unable to move on after three years or more, you need more than this book. Make for your GP for a chat and advice and maybe a spot of therapy or a spell on medication. Remember, everyone has their ups and downs, but there may come a point when you might need a little bit more, especially when a good night's sleep is not helping with your overwhelming feelings.

Have a look at these questions written for us by a GP, to give you an indication of whether a trip to the doc's would be a cunning plan:

- Do you have feelings of deep despair, which at the back of your mind you know are out of proportion to your situation?
- Are the negative feelings of loss and mourning getting worse as time goes by?
- Are you crying a lot?
- Are you sleeping badly?
- Are you worrying about your health or are you feeling unwell more than usual?
- Would you like to talk and understand more and more?
- Do you feel as though you've run out of puff from your friends and family and you now feel like a burden to them?
- Are you going round and round in circles in your head?
- Do you still need to talk excessively about your situation and pick over all the details to try to find some answers?

- Do you feel as though you're going through the process of accepting and dealing with your situation slowly?

You may answer 'yes' to the odd one of these questions, but answering 'yes' to a whole host of them might suggest that a little bit of professional help would be a good idea. There's nothing to be embarrassed about because it's not uncommon to need some extra help to come out the other side.

Smell the Air

Come on, poke your head out of the burrow, sniff the air and start to look forward and to dream again. It's time to review where you are now in the same way that a shop would do a stock-take before deciding which lines of clothing to dump and which are going to be the next thing. And if you need to be inspired, then here you are: A-list stars who reinvented themselves (and just happen to be single mums too!).

- Liz Smith became an actress at the age of 52.
- Thelma Barlow left *Coronation Street*, went to Hollywood and was voted at the Oscars as best newcomer at the age of 72.
- J K Rowling wrote some books over a latte that have done rather well.
- HRH Prince Andrew's ex-wife Fergie dropped four stone and went on to be the spokesperson for WeightWatchers, getting herself out of a monumental financial hole.
- Kate and Emily became TV talent and authors (though are yet to get out of a monumental financial hole!).

Some things that other single mums wanted to share, totally unprompted by us...

Don't give up on yourself – remember that if you act as though you're wonderful you will be. Reveal your innermost self.

We all think we'd like to be a 'normal, happy, married person'. But who are they? And are they really happy? And if they're happily married, maybe they would be just as happy single, and if we're unhappy single, maybe we'd be unhappy married.

Enjoy yourself when the children are with their dad At first it'll be hell, but learn to take pleasure being able to have a good sleep, go for a drive, meet friends, get a jigsaw on the go, watch telly, clean or have a drink.

Make your social life happen. Get a babysitter once a week and go out. If you're invited out, say 'yes' and put it in your diary in PEN and then go, no excuses, no backing out.

We hear time and time again about single mums who get a frisson of excitement as they realize they can do something different and unscripted with their lives and emerge re-invented. The first step to re-invention (or just a re-launch if you fancy hanging on to the current version!) is to reconnect with yourself by taking a long hard look in the mirror …

How Well-oiled Is Your Engine?

How well-oiled is my engine?! Yes! It's a slightly odd way of looking at how well you're doing, but when you think about it, the engine analogy makes perfect sense.

All aspects of our lives interconnect, just as cogs of an engine do. It's when all areas are trucking along nicely that our lives run sweet as a nut. If one cog packs up, the whole lot grinds to a halt. So indulge us: imagine the main parts of your life as cogs all working together to make a marvellous, greased-lightning sort of engine.

We've devised an MoT that you can complete after a jolly good look under your bonnet. This will help you get the various aspects of your life into some sort of balance. Have a go.

This MoT is for you to do once every few months, to show you what's working and to alert you to those areas that need some attention.

The things we look at are all to do with your life NOW. For help with future plans, have a look at Chapter 9 (Old Lives, New Lives). But for now, let's concentrate on the current state of play.

We've picked seven 'cogs' for your MoT. Give each of these parts of your life a score out of 10, where 10 means you've got it spot-on and 1 means 'dreadful'.

The Cogs

1. How you feel

Are you sailing nicely at the moment or is everything grinding you down? Are you exhausted, short-tempered and depressed? OK, we all have low times – it'd be weird for anyone not to, regardless of whether they're a single parent or not. But if you find that you're getting no enjoyment or fun from things that you would expect to, be it a night out with your pals or a session at the dogs, then alarm bells should be ringing and you should give yourself a lower score than if such a night out can still rally you and make you feel better. So, engine currently feeling ropey or up for anything?

MY SCORE OUT OF 10

2. Health and fitness

How well are you feeling? If you're feeling a tad on the large side, or just a bit sensitive or unhappy about having a wobblier tummy than the average, you might want to give yourself a lower score than if you feel you and your wobbles belong together and you'd honestly feel less happy without them. We should all, of course, aim to be as fit and healthy as we can be for all the obvious reasons, including being around for as long as possible to look after our children. So if buns, fags and bucket-loads of fine wine and alcopop chasers have become your staple diet, have a long hard look at yourself and consider your engine over-oiled – time to pull back!

Becoming a single parent can also knock your self-esteem and confidence, and feeling unhealthy, unfit or overweight won't help. So how much of a show do health and fitness make in this engine – do you feel good about yourself physically or would you like to improve your chassis?

MY SCORE OUT OF 10

3. Friends old and new

Friends are always important, but when you're single they can be even more so. We all need company, especially if the majority of our lives is spent with children. It's important to have one or possibly two great mates to be your trusted confidantes so you have somewhere to offload about how you really feel. You should have an outlet and not keep it all bottled up. But you also need people to play with and to just have fun with. Child-free weekends can be a real perk of being a single parent, but it's less of a perk if you don't have anyone you feel able to ring up and arrange to see on those weekends, or whom you can drag with you to the latest film, club, bridge evening, etc. You may have lots of friends but they may all be female, or all married and so not up to the same sorts of things as you. So how is your social scene looking? Nicely revved up or knocking a bit?

MY SCORE OUT OF 10

4. Family (not including you and the children)

They come in all shapes and sizes and can drive you mad, but they can also be a fantastic emotional and practical support: especially your parents, as they'll feel as protective and worried about you as you do about your own children. It's time to pull your extended family a little closer and to call on the men in your family to do a bit more of male-type stuff with your children. Family will help to remind you and your children that you're still anchored as part of a wider family unit. It's a reassuring feeling when you're beginning to feel a bit on your own and short-changed on the family front. However, divorce isn't necessarily going to bring out the best in you or your family. Watch your behaviour, manage theirs and try to maintain a good relationship. So how go relationships with the clan? Do you get the practical and emotional support that you need from them? Are you being too touchy or demanding with them?

MY SCORE OUT OF 10

5. Interests and hobbies

We want to encourage you to make sure you're developing beyond being a mother and a single parent. Do you have anything else to distract and absorb you? Can you spend time enjoyably? Emily went off to an evening class. Others have gone fitness-mad and become personal trainers or marathon runners, joined book clubs, film clubs, learned a language, taken a course to re-train in something that interests them. Even Kate got handy with the essential oils! We're after a state of mind where being a single mum is just a part of you and not the whole you. New interests and hobbies help you to feel more like yourself.

So, are your interests and hobbies enough to make you feel more than just a single mum?

MY SCORE OUT OF 10

6. Money

It doesn't matter how much you've got to live on, you still have to make sure you're living within your budget; if you don't, the worry and stress can be overwhelming. So when you start to think how well you're doing in terms of living within your means, bear in mind how often, and by how much, you go into the red. How in control of your finances do you feel? Are you in debt? Are you aware of some big bills coming up and have no idea how you're going to meet them? If you do have big bills but you've worked out a way of dealing with them, then give yourself a better score than if you've that tight, butterfly feeling about how you're going to pay them. Chapter 8 (Money Matters) goes into this area in loads more detail, but for now, assess your money cog – well oiled?

MY SCORE OUT OF 10

7. Love life

Those who know us will be very aware that we certainly don't believe that a boyfriend is the answer to everything (just as well in the current circs!). But having someone on your side who's good for hugs and isn't a child or relative is a nice thing to have. If we're honest we'd all like to be loved and the apple of somebody's eye, but there's no point even looking for a boyfriend if you're feeling too needy, still cut up about your separation and so on. You need to have dealt with this stuff first. So even if you've got a new squeeze, you may give your love-life cog a low score if you know it's all rebound stuff and you're running before you're ready to walk. There's a fine line between balancing the demands of boyfriend and children, which Chapter 9 (Old Lives, New Lives) investigates, but are you giving the new man enough of your time and energy? Are you balancing him, home and children well? Are you too dependent on him (or on the idea of him)? And if you're ripe for a bit of dating action – how are you doing on your quest? If you feel a long way off being able to date, then this is a low-scoring cog and will probably improve as 'how you feel' improves, so focus on the whole engine.

MY SCORE OUT OF 10

Did You Pass Your MoT?

Now work out your average score:

0 – 4	MoT fail, remedial action needed! Work out an action plan – focus on one or two areas you're able to handle at the moment, look for some easy wins.
5 – 6	MoT just scraped a pass. You need to invest some time working out how to improve your average.
7+	MoT passed with merit. Well done, you've got the easy wins, now start tackling the larger issues that will help to raise your MoT scores even further.
9+	Please forward secrets of success to Kate and Emily – share, share!!!

Remedial Action and Cranking It Up

One or two areas might stand out which are clearly out of kilter with the others. If you have a low score and are feeling particularly wobbly, with '2' for love life (though your friends and family are great and get a good score) and a bad score for fitness, you need to think of easy ways of upping the low scores so that when you return to this MoT in a few months' time or so you can see that things are improving or changing.

Below are some ideas of things you can do to help improve your MoT scores. Some will seem straightforward and simple (the easy wins) while others might have to be seen as more long term. Remember, though, these are just our ideas; you're very likely to have better ones yourself, so put your thinking cap on and start to set yourself some easy and some more challenging targets.

How you feel

If your score is very low this may say more about the situation than you. This could be the stage when you just need to make yourself feel better:

- Have a haircut.
- Get a massage, spa day or facial. If that's beyond your budget, put your feet in a washing-up bowl full of hot water and a drop or two of essential oils, light a candle and put on some relaxing music in a darkened room. That should do the trick.
- Sort out your house so that any mess or chaos stops bringing you down. Start with a drawer, a cupboard or even just a pile.
- Chuck away a load of horrible old clothes and buy one or two new things.
- Have at least two early nights a week (no one's going to know, so 8.30 p.m. is possible!).
- However rubbish or fat you feel, have three days in a row when you make an effort to look nice – wash and brush your hair, wear your nice clothes and make-up, polish your shoes. It's amazing how much better you feel once you make yourself make an effort (we know this for a fact!).

Health and fitness
- Do more walking or swimming, buy an exercise DVD or sign up for a marathon.
- Find a local yoga class.
- Cut down on the alcohol intake or have a spell on the wagon.
- If binge-eating is your thing and you have a penchant for crisps and other quality nibbles, DON'T buy them any more. (And don't kid yourself that you have them in the house for the children.)

Friends
Find people who like the same sorts of things as you do. Write a list of things you like doing or would like to try, and find a club devoted to it. Here are some ideas:

- book club
- bridge club
- adult education

- sports clubs such as tennis or golf
- wine appreciation groups
- creative writing groups
- film clubs
- charity work
- church groups.

Get out there and get social; make some plans when you're having an up moment:

- invite people round to yours
- see more of your neighbour
- organize a gang to go out with.

Family
- Try to make responsibility less of a solo mission by sharing it, first with your children's dad and then with other people in your family.
- You may feel like battling on completely on your own with an 'I can cope' mentality, but off-loading even a bit will be good for you:
  - Arrange a sleepover at the grandparents, or get them to take the children out on a trip or spend time looking after the children at home while you go out.
  - Invite the children's uncles and aunts over for games of football, model-making, etc., or ask them to join up with you and the children for a trip out.
- If you're taking it all out on your nearest and dearest, talk to them and tell them what's upsetting you. Apologize for your behaviour and ask them to cut you a bit of slack.

Interests and hobbies
- Think of things you used to do or that you always wanted to try. Even if now isn't the time to take them up, thinking of ideas is a step forward. Emily has promised herself a bit of beekeeping in quieter years to come, and she indulges in it a little already by

reading about it – odd, but true!

- Take up some solitary pursuits that you might like and could easily do on one of those pretty boring evenings in when the children are asleep. Kate is always happy when she has a jigsaw on the go.
- DVDs (you could get to know a particular producer's or actor's work to give it a bit more of an angle).
- Writing (they say we all have a book inside us!). Go on, DO IT.
- Surfing the Internet (loads to find. How about researching your family tree? flogging stuff on eBay?).
- Painting or drawing. Bring out the artist in you. Go on, get the children's art stuff out and have a go, it's great fun (which would be why children like it so much).
- Have you always meant to get involved in voluntary work? Well then, research, investigate, and join in.

Money

- Don't allow fear or worry to stop you from thinking about how to solve the problem.
- Open your post.
- Read your bills and statements so you understand them.
- Phone your bank (or get online banking) for an up-to-date balance.
- Talk to your bank and find out what they suggest and have to offer. Don't forget that although they're keen for you to take out loans, etc. they do have the ability to tell you if it would work out cheaper than paying interest on credit cards and overdraft fees.
- Review all suppliers and ask them for their cheapest tariffs.
- Read Chapter 8 (Money Matters).

Love life

There's a two-stage approach to this: making sure you're ready for it, and then going and getting it. So if your score is low here, you need to at least first make sure you can:

- Spend time on your own happily. Spend some fun evenings in, even reading the paper – the aim being to be able to be at home on your tod and to do it peacefully.

- Then there's your next decent child-free slot: think of things to entertain yourself with during these times.
- Get more social – invite friends round, meet up, become a social creature.
- People say it's a numbers game, so get as much exposure as you can handle!
- And of course, read Chapter 9 (Old Lives, New Lives) for more ideas.

Whatever you decide to do, make a plan, make it manageable, and make sure you keep pushing forward and a bit beyond what feels comfortable all the time.

Dear Kate and Emily,
I got married when I was 22 and that was 20 years ago! I got divorced five years ago and have spent much of that time focusing on the children. I now want to spend some time on me and I'm finding it so hard to get out there and develop my life. It feels so different from when I was last single and I really can't think how on earth to go back to that old life. It just doesn't feel like me any more.
Love,
Old Dog in Need of Learning New Tricks

Dear Old Dog,
Old dog, my foot! Nothing could be further from the truth, it just feels that way. Whether you're in your thirties, forties, fifties or sixties, there's loads of life still out there for grabs; there are people to meet, places to go and fun to be had. You've come to the right place for advice, as we too felt like a couple of

old dogs in need of learning new tricks, and boy, have we learned! Kate is a big one for courses and community groups, Emily is more of a bar-hopper and sports-club member, but probably the best thing we've done is working together on 'Kate and Emily', which is a great source of interest, passion and amusement for us. So why not find a cause or charity that you're passionate about and search for a way to join in and volunteer?

Once you get into the swing of meeting, mingling, interacting and having fun with new people, the dating scene will probably follow on naturally and seem less daunting. So rather than focusing on that horrid feeling of sitting on a dusty dating shelf when it doesn't feel natural any more, concentrate on everything else. The trick — concentrate on new things so that you feel more like a new dog with a new life, rather than an old dog at sea!

Love, Kate and Emily

❝ I've never felt so ashamed or embarrassed that I had to ask for help but it's the best thing I could have done. I wasn't well, I was miserable and it was the only thing to do for my little girls. I often think, why me? But I'm really still dead lucky. It's not a disaster. I'm not dead. I'm alive and I've two little beautiful girls at home. Don't get me wrong — it does get me down and I'm still on anti-depressants. But I don't feel sorry for myself. I have my off days, but who doesn't? ❞
Kerry Katona, *Daily Mirror* / Mirrorpix

Chapter 4

THE CHILDREN

As far as children go we really must make it clear that we've not got a single qualification between the two of us in this area (not even a Brownie childcare badge). We are, however, very good at collating common consensus, as well as listening to the experiences of everyone we've met and learning from talking to adults who experienced divorce as children.

And collating is pretty much what we've done for you in this chapter! We've distilled received wisdom (where we agree with it) and are sharing it with you here. We've added our own experiences and those of the people we've talked to.

If your children are having problems adjusting or coping and you feel you need more support, bob up to the GP, who should be able to refer you to a qualified and experienced professional in this field.

Whatever the age of your offspring, be they cute babies, trying toddlers or hormonal teenagers, it goes without saying that we all want the best for our fantastic children and that each stage provides its own 'special challenges'. We want to help the children develop into rounded and balanced adults. Our children are finding out, earlier than most, that life is not perfect. It's your job to make sure that they learn from the experience and still grow up to be well-adjusted and with their belief in love and family intact.

Grown-up lives and emotions are complex. You can argue the toss and still come to no conclusion. However, looking at situations through your children's eyes can give enormous clarity to the course of action you should take. This is because you're forcing yourself to put your children at the centre of your decision making and thinking, which is exactly where they should be.

'In retrospect I would be more mindful of the children
and less intent on my escape from the marriage.'
A Single Mum

So this chapter is all about the children and how we, as separated parents, can do our best to turn out happy adults. When working through this chapter, try and focus only on the children. Plant yourself firmly in their shoes. Look backwards and forwards from their perspective.

Have at all times lodged firmly in your brain the following list of needs children of any age may have. You can help give them these things through thought, word and deed, and not least your own behaviour:

- They will mind very much that this has happened. Although they may have friends whose parents are divorced and there seems to be loads of it around, they need help accepting and adjusting.
- They need some truth about what has happened, why and what it means to their lives. If you can't tell the whole truth, don't, but don't lie to them.
- They need to know that whatever has happened it's not their fault in any way, shape or form; they're not to blame.
- They have not been abandoned.
- They are loved and valued.

- Whatever has happened they're not expected, or even allowed, to take sides between Mum and Dad.
- The divorce is between parents, not child and parent.
- Mum is Mum and Dad is Dad; NOTHING can change that. Mum and Dad are their parents with all that that entails.
- They still have a family, it's just a different shape.
- Mum and Dad are not getting back together.
- They should be in no doubt about what will happen to them at every step.
- It's not bad to feel upset or sad.
- You appreciate their distress and will do all you can to help.

Through Your Child's Eyes

Considering what's best for your children can help you to see the wood from the trees, and the right or obvious thing to do. By thinking about your behaviour and decisions from a child's perspective you allow yourself some distance and view yourself and their dad rather remotely. This 'distance' helps to moderate your emotional and irrational responses and gives you the clarity to explain and defend your decision and actions.

So, looking from your child's perspective, how can you make things easier for them? Ask yourself:

- Is what I'm doing or saying to their dad really for the children's benefit? Or is it really to serve my own agenda and my own purposes?
- Is this more about me than about the children?
- Am I using the children to get back at him?
- How can the children have warm, wonderful childhood memories that make them feel secure and loved, if the two people they love most in the world are fighting (or worse still, trying to drag the children into the fight)?
- How will their big day at the school play feel for them if Mum and Dad are sitting under a black cloud in opposite parts of the hall?

- How can I expect them to enjoy their wedding or graduation if I haven't developed a grown-up method of being in the same place as their dad?
- Am I trying to get them to take my side?

Talking to Your Children about Your Separation

Children of any age can find it difficult to talk about how they feel about not living with both their parents. They say 'It's fine' or just don't talk about it. But general wisdom is that children benefit from talking about it – just like adults do. If they don't talk to you about it they can often get it wrong and think all sorts of things that would make your hair curl. So take the time to find out what they're thinking and help them through. It's worth bearing in mind that whatever was going on in your home prior to the split, it's probable that the actual separation will have come as an unwelcome surprise to the children, so assume nothing.

When looking around for advice in this area the phrase we've come across time and time again is 'Talk to children in an *age-appropriate* way.' However, examples of what this means are hard to find. But you know what happened, and you know your own children, so we're sure that if you bear the following pointers in mind you'll be able to think about the best, most age-appropriate way to talk to your children:

- What you say should be true.
- Explain what the split means to them in the short term: where they will live and so on.
- Offer an honest explanation as to why the split has occurred, but one which can't be construed in their minds as being their fault.
- You mustn't try to get them onside by alienating their dad.
- Make it clear that you understand their distress and that it's normal that they may be feeling very sad.
- Keep talking and going back to the subject. Never assume 'Phew wee, great, that's *that* conversation over and done with.'

Honesty and trust are vital. You can't tell them one thing until they're 18 and then tell them the truth because you think they're now 'old enough' – that, quite frankly, is asking for a HUGE backfiring session! Hard to imagine it working out well, child hugging parent and saying, 'Thanks for protecting me so well from such a horrid truth, I now feel well-adjusted enough to deal with it and will revise my feelings and attitudes towards you, Dad and love in the light of it. Thanks, wow, you're the best!' So, keep it basic and heavily simplify the complicated adult bit, keeping the nub of what really happened (or is happening) there so that what you say is true and will still be true when they're that 18-year-old.

Emily and her husband told their children, who were about five and four at the time:

> There are two types of love: one that a mummy and a daddy have for their children, which never, ever stops even when they're cross or even when they're very old. Then there's another type of love between grown-ups, and that sort of love you hope will last for ever, and sometimes it does and sometimes it just doesn't and it stops. And when it stops it's very, very sad and means that people can't live happily together any more, and that makes them and their children sad. So it's better for everyone if Mummy and Daddy live in different houses.

It's basic, but the good thing Emily's found is that because it's true and did reflect what was going on, this explanation still works for them, it has just become more sophisticated and been explained in more detail as they have got older.

Kate's children were very small when her husband left so she's had to address the subject since on a regular basis and is always amazed by the interpretation that the children have worked out for themselves which needs gently correcting all the time:

The last time I broached the subject it wasn't planned at all. We were at the end of a very long walk (I got completely lost on the coastal path!) in Cornwall and I said something along the lines of 'Is there anything you want to know about the divorce?' and my daughter said, 'Yes, but I don't like to ask you as I think it'll upset you. Will you tell me what happened?' So we had a lovely, gentle rehash over the whole thing, which was different to the previous talks we'd had when she was younger, and she took on a bit more information. My younger son, meantime, was listening and got completely the wrong end of the stick! Which took some while to sort out. So it's worthwhile learning from my mistake and ensuring you keep having private chats with each of your children separately.

> 'I told them with a carefully planned speech at a carefully planned time at the beginning of the holidays, so I could monitor their reactions long-term, when I knew that Dad's flat had been sorted out and when I knew I could say the words calmly without getting hysterical.'
> A Single Mum

It's true that children are resilient, but they're also capable of keeping an enormous amount inside. They say babies learn to smile first to hook us adults in by pleasing us. Pleasing grown-ups is a habit that's apparently hard to kick, and many children are so keen to keep Mummy and Daddy happy that they don't want to add to their worries with their own questions, or upset them even more by raising the subject. You see, they're NOT fine, so talk to them and help them to tell you their worries.

Helping You Talk to Your Children about Your Separation

Children have to be pretty old (and boys even older than girls) before they can identify and understand their own emotions. It's probably when they're teenagers that they start to come to grips with them, and even then they still need help. As a result children may not understand what it is they're feeling, so you can help them by naming it: for example, 'You might be feeling sad [or fed up, or very miserable] because you won't see Dad for another two weeks,' etc. An alternative is, 'Often children feel sad when their parents split up. Do you?' There are numerous variations on this theme, which we won't bore you with, as long as you've got the gist …

Try asking your children these questions, but pick your time (Emily finds hers like to tell her serious things at bath time or when they're being tucked up).

Be warned, they're bound to say that 'You getting back together' or 'Seeing Dad right now' would make them happier (or a shiny new bike, more pocket money, etc!). You can explain why that's not possible; the aim of this conversation is to try and help them by teaching them to manage being sad, angry, etc. – not to give in to demands!

Your checklist

- In the eye of the storm, children's needs should be paramount, not trapped between parents or go-betweens.
- Realize the differences between your feelings and the children's:
  - You might hate their dad, they love him.
  - You might feel like you've been let out of prison, they'll feel devastated.
- All the books and professionals say it: the most important factor in helping children handle divorce is the ongoing relationship they have with their mum *and* dad.
- Love your children as much as possible. Cuddle them.
- Listen to them and let them talk. Tell them it's OK to express their feelings.
- Tell them the divorce isn't their fault.
- Keep parenting consistent – don't over-compensate for the divorce, or take it out on the children.
- Research shows that it's good for children if parents can keep their parenting style after separation consistent with how it was pre-separation.

- It's important for children to keep their relationships going with both sides of the family (grandparents, aunts, uncles, cousins).
- You need to roll with the punches; there will be setbacks and upsets. The key is not to let them overwhelm you and get back on track ASAP.
- Try to limit the amount of change in children's lives at any one time.
- Do you love your children more than you hate their dad? Well then, put them first!

Dear Kate and Emily,

Let's be frank – my husband left me for a lap-dancer, and not just any lap-dancer – she's a he! I clearly can't talk to the children about it, it's not for their ears and I most certainly won't be telling them that Dave (aka Delilah) is their father's new love interest. What's on my mind, though (other than the obvious!), is the children hearing about it from someone else, or what to say if they ever overhear me and a friend talking. At the moment I'm just protecting them from the whole sordid affair. Any advice?

Love,

Keeping Stum of Keithley

Dear Keeping Stum,

It's a shocker how children talk, spread gossip and pick up the proverbial fag-end. There's nothing worse as an adult than being the last to know something, is there? We can all surely cite some instance of being very miffed when we were the last to know that someone was pregnant or dating that bloke off the telly, etc. So imagine how your children will feel if they're the last to know about their dad and the gossip that'll no doubt surround his 'colourful' departure. We know of people who've never forgiven their mothers for keeping stum about such matters. You must pre-empt this situation, as it'll happen as sure as night follows day. You must be truthful — just remember that irritating phrase, 'age-appropriate'.

Reassure them that Dad loves them, that he's still Dad and that everyone is an individual and what other people say is not important. Provide them with some responses to the teasing and have a word with the school. Teasing is a form of bullying and the overwhelming majority of schools will have an anti-bullying policy. At the end of the day your children will learn that we're all different, that families are different, but that what really matters is love and kindness and that their family (though not the norm) is a great place to be. And if people can't understand that, then that's their problem. If they don't know about lap-dancers, call Delilah 'a dancer', and if they've not heard of gay, then tell them about it. If this is all too hard and painful for you (we wouldn't be at all surprised!), then get their dad to explain it. And if he can't/won't? Then ask another adult whom you trust to be as kind, sensitive and gentle as possible. Good luck and be brave, they deserve to hear about all of this at home, and we think they would benefit from a bit of armour against the teasing.

Love, Kate and Emily

Let Children Be Children

Don't forget your children are always your children, however old they are. This is a different relationship from friend or confidant. This child/parent relationship shouldn't change as a result of you no longer being with their dad. Don't encourage the children to fill their dad's place as friend and confidant. It's not fair; children of any age need to have boundaries set by parents and need to know exactly where they stand. Making them child, friend and confidant combines too many conflicting roles. So whatever the shape of this family, don't lose sight of the fact that you are the parent.

What you share with them needs to be age-appropriate. Even if they're teenagers and look like grown-ups, they don't need burdening with Mum's adult issues and tales from the boudoir! Watching someone's life fall apart on *Eastenders* is one thing; your mother revealing all sorts of weaknesses and insecurities is quite another.

We know that being single again can bring on a re-blossoming as mumsy clothes are traded in for the latest fashion and you rediscover bars, men and single life again. However, this is your children's first crack at being young and single, and at least your second! So be gracious and allow them the limelight. Please don't compete with them over clothes, clubbing and boyfriends, as you're still Mum. Do your single stuff off their patch.

Never make your son the man around the house. True, you want to teach him to grow up to be a man, but there's a distinction between being the 'little man' and being responsible for things that adults are supposed to do. Your child shouldn't be your confidant, escort or your rescuer. Correct people if they suggest that now your son 'is the man around the house' or that he should 'take care of Mummy', and help take the pressure off him by replying along the lines of, 'Oh, there's no need for that! He's being a lovely boy!'

Behaving Like Adults in Front of the Children

Always remember that your children will only ever have one mother and one father. They will unconditionally love both and want both, warts and all. They'll be incapable of stopping loving you both, whatever you do to each other. However, it's possible to turn a child against either of its parents; this is called Parental Alienation Syndrome (PAS). This is a cruel and selfish thing to do and is achieved essentially by sustained brainwashing, making the child hate, distrust and/or have such extremely negative thoughts towards one of their parents that they may end up refusing all contact. Words can't express how appalled we feel about behaviour of this sort, however subtle it may be, and quite rightly the courts take any evidence of it happening extremely seriously.

Remember, the way children observe their parents behaving towards each other will have an effect on:

- how happy they are (children hate to see conflict between parents)
- how torn they feel (they'll feel like you're asking them to take sides, which goes against all of their natural instincts)
- how easily they can talk to you (they can't tell you they're worried about what it means to them when their dad's getting married if they know you hate talking about him)
- how much they internalize their fears/worries (doing this just makes them worse – we all know that)
- how they learn to behave as part of a couple in future years.

Underlying everything we do at 'Kate and Emily' is the fundamental belief that we do what we do for the wellbeing of ALL of our family (us and our children). Our children ground us, and looking at things through their eyes helps us to behave more like adults and to keep our pride and self-respect intact. Of course our children aren't in clover about the whole thing, but we can at least have homes where they feel able to tell us what they think and feel.

How Are You Doing?

Here are some questions to help you to take a look at how you're doing at the moment. The answers might help you to change tack a bit, keep on trucking, or reverse at speed and start again!

Remember there's always a point to fixing things – even if only for damage limitation. 'Can't' is not an acceptable answer.

Do You ...

A   let slip in front of the children that their dad is a scheming, tight-fisted, money-grabbing good-for-nothing?

B   keep things as normal as you can by keeping to the old routine and trying to protect them by saying to yourself, 'They'll understand when they're 18 and I can tell them then'?

C   explain human frailty and that, however fickle love between adults can be, it's always a constant and never changes regardless of circumstances between a parent and their child?

If Your Child Were in the Lead Role at the School Play, Would You ...

A   not tell their dad about it so he doesn't go?

B   invite him but do your best to keep your distance during the performance and during the interval by giving him a very wide berth?

C   save a seat for him so you could sit together, so your child doesn't have to worry and they can just bask in the knowledge that you're both there to cheer them on?

When It Comes to Their Dad's Family, Do You ...

A   keep your ex's family well out of the picture, refusing to talk about them or pass on any family stories about them or their dad to the children?

B   send them birthday and Christmas cards from the children, but be buggered if you're going to sign them too?

C   carry on with them pretty much as normal (e.g. talking to the children about them, phoning them for a quick chat and then passing them over to the children)?

Do You Ever Ask the Children ...

A   'Has Dad got a new squeeze then? Is she horrid and ugly?'

B   'How was your weekend at Dad's? What did you get up to?' And then react to the answer by saying how irresponsible he was to allow them to be out so late, stay up late, swim without armbands, watch an 18 film etc., etc.

C   'Did you have a lovely time? What did you get up to? Ohh, that sounds fun! No wonder you're tired – let's get you bathed and in bed!'

If you answered mainly ...

As   Reverse at speed!

Bs   You're with the majority – well done, you're going in the right direction. You just need to have a look at where there's still room for improvement and make some changes.

Cs   Blimey! Well done! Maintain top performance.

It's Not All Doom and Gloom

There's no doubt that being brought up in a single-parent household means that, in a very practical way, you take on more as a child:

- Your mother has only one pair of hands. If she's doing one thing, she can't do what you need, like getting your coat out of the cupboard, remembering that it's swimming at school and what you need to take, etc.
- You understand money and saving up for things and that you can't have it all.
- You're a part of the team with your mum, and help with DIY and housework. It's more of a joint venture.
- You help to look after younger siblings.
- You take responsibility earlier.
- You look after yourself sooner.
- The adult world meets your childhood world sooner.
- You get the chance to have the adult world explained to you by a loving parent.
- You're a closer unit because you have to do things together – your mum can't leave one child at home while she shops or takes another child to Brownies – one goes, you all go.

Yes, separation and divorce are difficult and the knock-on effects multiply. But they can, and often do, lead to more stable and satisfying relationships within the family. We've often heard parents *and* children say how they feel they know each other better because they spend more quality time in each other's company.

We've heard people look back fondly on their childhoods, admiring their mum for how she managed to keep it all going, and still found time to love them and bring them up well!

Emily reassures herself that her children's rather earlier-than-hoped-for introduction to the grown-up world isn't in itself a worry, as long as she keeps the atmosphere in the house happy and tries to make home a nice place to be. The key to that seems to be telling herself to chill out when she can feel the stress rising!

Kate believes that the relationship she has with her children (and their childhood) would've been very different had the good ship *Marriage* remained at sea. As she says:

> there'd probably have been more children and more material possessions. However, the positives of a really, really close, fabulous relationship between the three of us and the integration of other people outside the family into our orbit are huge. Our friends bring such colour, along with an understanding that things and people can be different and that's OK, and these are good things that I don't underestimate.

“ The children become the weapon and the shield. The weapon is: 'If you do this to me you won't see your children.' So one party has no control. And the shield is: 'Please don't do this to me because I won't let the children see you.' Give me this or you won't see the children; don't do this to me or you won't see the children. The children become the weapon and the shield. Remove this from the battleground – because it is a battleground. Make this area neutral. **”**
Bob Geldof, 17th June 2002, Shared Parenting Information Group

Chapter 5

CO-PARENTING

The benefits to the children of having parents who co-operate are enormous, and the negative effects of parents who don't behave towards each other in a civil way are far-reaching. We want you to work towards mending or reforming your relationship with the children's dad. This isn't about making you like or respect him, but about *accepting* the fact that you've got to work together on a joint mission and with common aims for the sake of the children. As the adults we have to make it happen by co-parenting.

Co-parenting is exactly what it says on the tin: bringing up your children together as a mother and a father, working together and co-operating to do the best you can for your offspring. We feel that in their heart of hearts, whoever did what to whom and why, most people believe it's a good idea for their children to have a relationship with both parents, and that this will help them grow into well-rounded adults. Mothers and fathers raise their children together; that is the way we humans do it. While it's undoubtedly easier to bring up the children when you live together, just because you're no longer with their dad, your children needn't be denied the love, care and attention of both of you.

In this chapter we aim to give you the desire, the attitude and the tools to turn the goal of co-parenting into a reality.

Emily's co-parenting arrangement with her ex-husband involves him having the children on alternate weekends. Emily and her ex also alternate Christmases, and the children spend as many bank holidays and school holidays with their dad as possible. Kate does more of an Andy-and-Fergie routine based around the old marital home she still shares with the children. In her case the children's father joins them for part of every weekend, and twice during the week he does bath/bedtime and homework. He lives a short distance away. They also manage to spend time and holidays *en famille* from time to time.

These very different approaches work for them and theirs at the moment. It's up to both parents to agree a realistic, achievable way of managing their own situation. So read on and pick out the bits that will work best for you.

Setting up a co-parenting plan is not so much a self-help task with a vague aim; it's more of a nuts-and-bolts thing. Think business plan, think strategy. We know that when the going is fraught and emotional (as it often can be), the way to stay in control and on track is to take the emotion out of the exercise and draw up your plan in a business-like way. Look at the topics we discuss in this chapter and then fill in your own co-parenting plan. When you've filled it in, read your answers out loud and question yourself about them, and keep coming back to the plan as your thoughts become clearer.

The objective of the co-parenting plan is to create an agreement that will keep you and the children's dad clear about how you intend to bring them up together. It can be a bit of a dry old subject, but so many people have found our plan a help that we thoroughly recommend using it.

Stop the War!

When the proverbial s*@"! hits the fan, it's unrealistic to expect everyone to behave well. This isn't like your break-ups with boyfriends in the past; so much more was invested and lost this time. And to make it even worse, you can't cut the tie or badmouth your ex until you no longer care. This one you've got to face and deal with for one very simple reason: if you don't, the children will be made pawns, used as weapons, and will ultimately suffer.

We bet that you've felt at least three of the following emotions since starting on the single-parent road:

- shock and disbelief
- fear and panic
- embarrassment and failure
- betrayal and bitterness
- mistrust or disappointment
- anger or guilt
- moral superiority or the feeling of being trampled.

If we're right, then it's also likely that you've found yourself doing something along these lines:

- shouting and wailing
- justifying your own poor behaviour
- being spiteful or petty
- seeking martyrdom
- being nasty, bloody-minded or indifferent
- blaming others
- kicking car doors, slamming doors in faces and possibly even biting?!

... Oops!

There's a point when you know you're out of control and need to change something: what about the woman who found herself peering through the privet hedge to get a glimpse of her ex-husband's new home, saw the photos of him and his new girlfriend on the mantelpiece and only then began to be appalled at what she was doing?! Then there's the mother who did something quite unpleasant to her ex-husband's and his new girlfriend's toothbrushes – use your imagination! Children have been ripped off parents in the street; abuse has been hurled at the new girlfriend when the ex-wife and she have bumped into each other in the supermarket, and passers-by have had to break up fights. When you've reached a level of behaviour that's a tad on the embarrassing side, or verging on the illegal, it's definitely time to stop the war!

We won't go into our own bad behaviour too much here, though Kate remembers an occasion when her mother said to her, 'We don't do that to anyone in this family. You weren't allowed to as a child and you certainly won't do it as an adult, so you're going to have to apologize for that NOW.' Kate knew then that she'd gone too far and that just because she felt mightily pissed off and tired, it didn't give her the right to lose her grip completely. It was a wake-up call from a normally supportive mother, and Kate had to come up with a new approach to her own co-parenting.

Emily, on the other hand, has always kept a lid on any of this sort of behaviour and emotional stuff (Kate would say too tight a lid!) since she felt so guilty about the break-up. So she bent over backwards to be as accommodating and reasonable as she could, which isn't always ideal as you can just as easily forget to put the children's needs first as you can when you're fighting ('No, no, I quite understand if you need three years' travelling in Outer Mongolia to get over the hurt and find yourself again. The children will be absolutely fine, don't worry; trot off and have fun.'). Not of course that her husband fancied Outer Mongolia – but you get the gist. Our co-parenting form can help to shift the focus away from guilt and anger and on to the practicalities of how to co-parent best.

Please realize that it's mortifying to look back on your own bad behaviour, so if you're currently in the 'breakupville war zone', make sure you only hurl things around when the children aren't there, and try to work towards a point of indifference.

Dear Kate and Emily,
My husband and I had a deeply acrimonious divorce, and
although it seems long ago (eight years) it was a very, very bad
time. We both said some terrible things and have both behaved
badly. Although both he and I have been involved in the children's
upbringing it has been made difficult by the fact that we've kept
up the point-scoring, the bitching and the petty behaviour and
our new partners are involved behind the battle lines as well. To
be honest, my problem is knowing how to stop this. I can't go on
fighting with him any more, I'm tired, worn out and depressed by
it. I just want it to stop and know that it's not going to start
again. How do I go about this? He'll just wipe the floor with me;
it's probably easier to argue. I know he's a good dad and, to be
honest, a decent man, but we seem to have become enemies now
and the thought of that continuing really brings me down.
Love,
Want a Truce in Truro

Dear Want a Truce,
You're halfway there just wanting to stop, and remember, no one
can have a fight with themselves — they need a willing adversary!
You can declare a truce unilaterally and follow a code of conduct
that you believe in. Even if he doesn't sign up to the truce, it'll
give you a feeling of control and self-respect. It helps you to police
your own behaviour and takes the fight out of the situation. But
the most important factor is that the benefits to the children
will be great. Not only will they have your behaviour as a fantastic
role model; it's also highly likely that it'll rub off on their dad and
you'll be leading by example. We would recommend contacting him
and letting him know that you feel like this and that you'd like to
draw a line and start again. We're not suggesting barbecues and
barn dances, but if you follow a code of conduct you'll be able to
re-establish a good functioning relationship that won't only make

you feel better but will benefit your children enormously. So well done, go for it, it's really, really worth it, just imagine how much you can all enjoy future events such as weddings and grandchildren if the battle is over.

Love, Kate and Emily

Redefining Your Relationship

The separation process trains parents to think of each other as adversaries. You may have started off amicably but the lawyers can put a spanner in the works. Remember your lawyer saying something like 'You could get much more than that' or 'You don't need to agree to that much'? They're doing their job (and they may be right), but their job is to do the best for you, not for the *pair* of you. The whole process stokes the fire of confrontation.

To co-parent you need to shelve these confrontational weapons of mass destruction. Here are the pros and cons of waving the white flag and calling a truce:

Pros
- Peace is good for you.
- Harmony is good for the children.
- It'll make co-parenting a lot easier.
- You're both parents so he won't go away; life could be much less stressful if you call a truce.
- If you keep the battle going, he may well lose any interest in co-parenting and, trust us, you don't want that.

Cons
- You may secretly be hanging on to your former relationship, and being nice makes it harder to recognize it's over.
- Pretending everything's OK between you feels deceitful and fake,

and having a fight helps you to feel better about leaving.
• Having to be nice to someone who left you is incredibly hard – why should they get away with it?

We feel the pros outweigh the cons and show just how important it is to stop the war. So next task is to start to work towards a truce, and stop the war.

Now here is a very simple concept to get your head around. Think of someone with whom you've a good and functional relationship. You know the type: someone you've got to co-operate with to achieve what you want in a non-confrontational way. For example:

• a work colleague
• your child's teacher
• your bank
• your doctor
• a traffic warden about to give you a ticket.

Imagine using the same language, tone of voice and manner that you might with these people when you talk to your ex. You give just enough information or help to get the job done and you don't share anything irrelevant. Oh, and you say everything very nicely.

Kate knows for a fact that if she were to barge into Dr Sick Note's surgery *demanding* treatment for her bunions in an aggressive way it would be highly unlikely that she'd get the best out of the doc. She also knows for a fact that if she swears at Ms Detention the teacher, she'll make life very difficult for herself and her children.

Emily realized that to get off a parking fine she needed to be diplomatic, present her case clearly (she rather anally annotated a photocopy of a parking permit) and keep her views on the council tricking innocents like her into paying astronomical fines to herself! Bright cookie! She got off the fine.

In these examples it's easy to see how impossible it is to get things done if you don't behave properly and calmly and stick to the agenda

– because if you didn't, there'd be an almighty confrontation and argument and you'd have achieved nothing positive. So why then would you imagine that behaving like this with your children's dad is going to get the results you want?

Here are some top tips that will help you and their dad to keep things under control:

- Give each other loads of space.
- Go at the speed of the person most hurt by the split.
- Let each other have time to work through bad feelings.
- Be polite and courteous.
- Be punctual for arrangements.
- Stick to a relevant and appropriate agenda.
- Think before you speak.
- Have a cooling-off period when you get overheated.
- Follow through to show you can be trusted.
- Put things in writing and agree action points.
- Work out a code of conduct carefully.
- Keep your dignity and self-respect.

Dear Kate and Emily,
I'd really love to get my head around the idea of co-parenting, but I can't see any way that it could ever be possible! Come on, my ex and I HATE each other. He's a manipulative, selfish, destructive, arrogant, bullying bastard and he takes me to court on any pretext. He bribes the children to spy, he stalks me, he takes the children from school without letting me know before-hand and he insults me in the street. Now tell me to co-parent! You can stuff that, and him, where the sun don't shine. The sooner we're shot of him the better; he brings nothing but aggro and spite to the party.
Love,
Extremely Toxic of Tavistock

Dear Extremely Toxic,

This is all about ending a cycle, disarming, and starting again. From this base you may be able to co-parent effectively, which would be great for the children and would make your life 100% easier and less stressful.

It's true sometimes the fighting between warring parents is incredibly vicious, harmful and emotionally damaging. It's not the norm, but it does happen and our advice can sound very flippant and naïve when you're in such an appalling situation.

You probably find it hard to look beyond the next (or current) court battle. But you must, because, like it or not, you two are bound together by your children and they're no doubt caught up in the mess, and will be very upset by it all. If you're in a situation that is so extreme that normal rules of civil behaviour don't apply and the cycle of abusive behaviour is impossible to stop, just listen to this. We know a couple of single mothers who found that getting a decent physical distance between them and their ex-husbands helped to break the incredibly destructive bond between them, and allowed them both to get the space they needed to become independent and rational people again. For example, one did it to get away from the emotional bullying that caused her health to deteriorate dangerously. She was moving away from an extremely toxic relationship with her children's father. But, and this is VITAL, she made sure that the father still had contact with the children and spent holidays with them. It's not ideal by any means, but it gives the parents a better chance of focusing on the children and parenting rather than fighting each other. But please only consider putting physical distance between the children and their father if there's NO other alternative.

Love, Kate and Emily

Avoid the trap (which many people seem to fall into) of thinking, 'A working relationship with my ex is impossible.' Many times we've heard people say things along the lines of 'If I'd been able to be civil or even friendly, we'd still be together.' This is a cop-out! A successful romantic partnership is wonderful, great, challenging and intense. Just because this is no longer possible with your ex doesn't mean that a business-like relationship with him is doomed. Create new roles for yourselves as partners in the business of bringing up your children.

Filling Out the Co-parenting Plan

It's now time to take you through the areas of co-parenting that you need to discuss with your children's dad and make decisions about before finalizing your co-parenting plan. The full plan is on pages 92–98, and is designed for both parents to fill out. We developed it out of our own experiences and those of other single parents we've spoken to. However, one size doesn't fit all – you may need to alter or add to it to make it suitable for your own particular set up. Feel free to do so; whatever works for you is fine by us. You should also review the plan together at regular intervals, aiming for every six months to start with. When it becomes second nature to co-parent like this, your reviews can be more fluid, as and when the need arises.

We'll take you through the plan section by section, discussing the things you might think about before answering each one. Be honest with your answers, as nothing is gained from secrecy or leaving things unsaid.

Be realistic

Above all, be realistic: don't over- or under-promise, or expect too much or too little of their dad. Think about how you're behaving as parents towards each other from all angles and from different perspectives. Put yourself in your mum's shoes – what would she say about how you're behaving and parenting together? Then your best friend's shoes –

what would s/he say? And most importantly, what would Kate and Emily say?! Looking at things through other people's eyes can help you to see what you should be doing more clearly.

Kate's Top Tip

Presumably you've inside knowledge about their dad that you've gleaned from your time together. You need to be very grown-up and avoid using this just to set him up for a fall or to get into an argument so you can gloat and show him up. If you do, chances are he'll probably fail and then back to square one you all go. Instead, use this inside info to the greater good. For example:

> I know their father has a bit of a temper, which can easily flare up, especially if he's tired and feels he's being hassled. I know his job is demanding and isn't very flexible. If I were to say to him, 'Can you be at a football tournament on Friday at 1.30, your son expects you to be there?' I'd be putting him under a lot of pressure and would be likely to get a negative (and potentially explosive!) response.
>
> But I also know that he's not completely unreasonable and will respond to a sensible suggestion, without undue pressure or an implied threat. If I put it differently and say, 'I won't tell the lad, but can you try and make the football? It's a tournament and so it's a better use of your time, rather than taking the afternoon off for a 20-minute match,' I'm likely to get a good result.

How Emily Keeps Her Expectations under Control

> The hardest thing about the co-parenting plan is de-personalizing it and taking your feelings out of the equation. I managed to do it by telling myself that these were conversations I was having on behalf of the children, so I was their representative. It made it all a lot clearer for me when I thought about it in terms of what the children could expect from us, rather than what I could expect from my ex-husband.

1. How Are You Going to Behave towards Each Other?

The purpose of encouraging you to think about your behaviour is to help you keep this new relationship with your ex within acceptable boundaries, and to keep the dialogue between you business-like, direct and focused on the children. It's the same as drawing up a code of conduct between you. This might sound a bit forced, but it only takes a teensy thing to knock the project off course, so we recommend maintaining tight control, particularly if you're currently in a toxic relationship.

If you go to a pub, you might see a code of conduct behind the bar that states how the landlord expects you to behave, and what they deem to be unacceptable behaviour that will get you barred. And we all remember the signs around the sides of the swimming pool showing us how to behave, even though it took Kate a while to figure out what 'no petting' meant!

It makes sense to do the same for co-parenting and draw up your own code of conduct, stating what sort of behaviour you expect of each other, and what's absolutely out of bounds. We know this is a good idea because numerous single parents, in different situations, have told us that they wish there was one they could refer to and give to their children's dad!

To draw up your own code of conduct stating how you intend to behave towards their dad, you first need to decide how you'd like him to behave towards *you*. Then (very important), ask yourself if you can behave like this, too – don't ask anyone to behave in any way that you're incapable of or are not prepared to!

Be realistic, be flexible, be kind and be supportive. Don't make unreasonable demands or have overly high expectations like 'Never be late (or early!) to get the children,' or 'Be charm personified at all times.'

Steer clear of flashpoints

By flashpoints we mean topics that are not to be discussed as they make either one of you uncomfortable and defensive. In the interests of making co-parenting as painless and successful as possible, these are clearly off the agenda. Not everyone has no-go areas; it probably depends on your history, how things have changed since, and how long ago your split was. But many do, and they can include:

- Personal comments: 'I can't believe you're going clubbing at your age – saddo!'
- How money's spent: 'How much did that bright red flashy penis extension parked on your drive cost? The one you call a "babe-magnet"?'
- How the new squeeze is different from your old one: 'Oh, Jed is soooo different from you, he's passionate, really funny and we're never up before lunch! Which of course he cooks; he's an absolute marvel.'
- Details of any sexual conquest or pick-up – you know the stories you tell your mates, but not necessarily an ex: 'Phew wee, what a stud! Eat your heart out, he's mine!'
- Unconfirmed plans: 'Oh, we're thinking of adopting like Brad and Angelina.'
- Lessons learned from your past relationship: 'I'll never work such long hours again, I'm not going to let *this* marriage fall apart!'

Carry it through

Keep to this way of behaving towards each other for as long as is humanly possible. It's surprisingly easy to undo all your good work by falling into a false sense of security and straying into danger areas, such as chewing over the history of your failed relationship.

And don't forget – signing up to a code of conduct is not about making you like or respect their dad; it's to do with accepting that you've got to work together as parents for the sake of the children.

Try, try, try, try and don't lie. To make your co-parenting plan work you need to build up some trust in this one common area of your lives.

2. Your Parenting Objectives

Although this may seem woolly and open-ended, it's important as it focuses your mind on the endgame. It's good for both parents to know what they're thinking about and it's also likely to make you both remember that ultimately you want the same thing: happy, healthy, well-balanced children.

It's great to be reminded that whatever has gone before, you're both on the same side when it comes to your children. And if at the moment it just makes you weep and reminds you of how awful it is for your children, then take a deep breath, put the plan to one side while you deal with the history, and get yourself in a more forward-looking frame of mind.

The short-term objectives that you might want to achieve as a parent over the next year will include things you're worried about and working on, such as:

- helping the children with their school work
- settling them into a new school or nursery
- finding childcare
- being around for them more
- helping them to become more confident socially
- teaching them how to handle the teenage world
- supporting their hobbies and interests
- helping them with applications for colleges.

Their dad might not have thought about these objectives but it's useful to get his views on them. Don't forget – no one else, other than their dad, is as interested in your children as you are. This means that he may be the best sounding-board for discussions about how to support little Johnny at school, or support his love of Warhammer models, or buy his first car.

Here's another light-bulb moment from Emily:

I was getting to the end of my tether trying to teach the children how to control their tempers, with pictures of them in bare-knuckle fights with policemen continually flashing across my mind. I mentioned it, almost as a last resort, to their dad and he just said, 'I was like that at their age. I'll talk to them about it.' Why did it never occur to me before to ask him? It's more than just the colour of their hair they get from him; it's some characteristics, too. Of course he's an obvious person to talk to about their behaviour! As Homer Simpson would say, 'Doh!'

3. Parenting Areas to Discuss with Each Other

Your children will probably be brought up exposed to the ins and outs of two different homes. Each home will have a different feel, atmosphere, look and rules. What goes on in the other home is something you can't control. However, in order to make it as easy as possible for everyone, both parents should have a reasonable idea of what's going on in the other home, if only to better understand their children's lives. For example, the day-to-day things that are acceptable or expected in each house, such as types of behaviour tolerated, punishments that will be doled out, rules, bedtimes, food, language, recreational activities and so on. The list is endless.

There are also some areas where it might make sense if both parents can agree and present a united front for the benefit of all. This is when you can join together and avoid being played off against each other. If you can reach agreement on things like sex, drugs and rock 'n' roll, or pierced ears, mobile phones or whatever is the hot topic of the moment, so much the better.

Education is another area that benefits from common agreement, and ditto if tricky medical decisions need to be made – it's good to have both Mum and Dad totally up to speed: for heck's sake, the child's allergic to penicillin!

Having said all that, we've slightly different takes on why letting their dad know what goes on in your home is a good idea. Kate feels that by discussing what happens in each house, the parents can incorporate tips, advice and rules from the other house into their own regime. For example, if she knows that the children are expected to make beds and help around the house at their dad's, then she'll get them into the habit of doing do it at her home, too, so that the children don't have to leap from A to B with two totally different sets of rules.

Emily agrees up to a point. She has seen the benefits of talking about the different house rules with their dad as it has meant they can share parenting advice on how best to discipline their children, how to avoid meltdowns, etc. And perhaps even more importantly from her perspective, it's given her a much better understanding of the children's 'other life', which helps in understanding them more completely. But Emily doesn't see two homes and two sets of rules as being so confusing for the children. They seem to slot in and out of each home easily without any confusion. Emily's view is that as long as it's clear to them that Mum's rules are Mum's rules and Dad's are Dad's, then everyone knows where they stand, children slot into each home and the potential to be played off against each other is nipped in the bud. The answer to 'But Dad lets us,' is 'Dad might, but you don't do that here.'

Regardless of our differing views, we both agree that these discussions about each home are not about you trying to alter what goes on in both. You can make your views known, and just like any good co-parent should, we're sure their dad will give them full consideration. But if he decides to carry on as he has been because it suits, then tough bananas.

Areas to discuss your views on might include:

- the level of independence the children should have
- performance/behaviour at school
- disciplining bad behaviour
- exposure to films, computer games and the Internet.

In addition, there are the practical aspects of parenting, the day-to-day elements that impact on both homes. Examples would be:

- getting homework done at weekends
- washing and ironing uniforms so they're ready for the week
- letting each other know how tired and emotional the children are and recommending quieter weeks/weekends
- telling each other about any ups and downs in the children's lives (falling out with their best friend, etc.).

4. Communicating with Their Dad

The success of your co-parenting plan will depend to a large extent on establishing good communication – between you and their dad and between him and the children. Agree between you the best way to convey different types of information and then set up the most effective, user-friendly and workable channels. You know the children's routines better and what's likely to be most popular with them. Share your recommendations and ideas with their dad.

We'll come on to methods of communication, but first a quick health check:

Do you walk into a given situation expecting to be offended? If so, you may find that you're subconsciously determined to find fault with anything and everything that's happening. Are you a little too quick to personalize any act or comment? Or are you a victim, accountable for nothing? Both these types of behaviour will make it difficult for anyone else to talk to you or deal with you or achieve anything constructive.

What's your preferred way of sorting out issues such as:

- day-to-day stuff about your children? Examples: 'Nelly's got nits so keep the bobble hat on' or 'Rose just won't stop eating plants, so keep an eye on her in the garden and try to nip it in the bud.'
- concerns about your children such as their health, education or behaviour?
- long-term plans for your children (e.g. schools, college)?
- the logistics of the children's time spent at their dad's?
- your own plans – new partner, new job, new home, etc.?

For some people it's email, and in particular email to the workplace, so that any discussions about your divorce, new partners and children stay out of the home. It'll mean that new partners are less likely to get dragged into discussions about divorce, maintenance and so on, and you'll be less likely to feel influenced or compromised. Because it's your workplaces and not your home, you may each feel calmer and more reasonable. You know yourselves and each other. It may be that one or both of you feels that having your personal life encroach on your work life is not a great idea. In which case maybe just use emails for confirming non-contentious arrangements like 'I'll drop them off at 6 on Friday.' Then for bigger subjects such as arranging holidays, a phone call might work best. Book a time in advance and tell their dad what you'd like to speak to him about. You can also try texting to set up a convenient time to talk on the phone. Mobiles also have the advantage of caller ID, so you can decide whether to pick it up if it's an OK time to talk, or leave it to ring and call back later.

And of course there's that old-fashioned method of sitting down and talking things through face to face, with coffee, beer, wine, stiff G-and-T or peppermint tea in hand – take your pick!

We both have different preferences: Kate is a keen emailer and finds it works a treat, especially with the odd follow-up phone call (to his workplace). Emily prefers doing schedules at drop-off time, then pre-arranged telephone calls for more lengthy discussions. If there's something that's more of a hot potato (like how you both deal with children's behaviour), then she feels going out for a drink or meal (a pretty short and early evening) works best as it gives more time to discuss things properly. A big plus is that it's also neutral territory, and being surrounded by fellow punters should ensure a decent level of behaviour all round.

Emily's top tip is to book time to talk to each other. It doesn't have to be much time or too formal, but when you only see each other for about ten minutes once every two weeks it's impossible to have a full discussion about the children. And believe her, things fester on both sides if they're left unsaid.

In the end, the method you choose will depend not only on what you're discussing but also on how good your relationship is.

5. Keeping Children in Touch with Their Dad

You can help their dad to stay in regular contact with the children by keeping him up to date on their daily routines and giving him times when they're most likely to be around and not too busy or tired to talk to him. Consult the children and find out what they'd like, but manage their expectations (it might be impossible for him to phone at 4.30 every day!). What they want might not work for their dad, but it can go into the pot and help you both work out an achievable plan. Be sensible about this plan and make realistic promises. Check that your suggestions are workable by thinking back over recent weeks and seeing if you would have liked him to call every Wednesday – isn't that the day you go swimming?!

If you can't guarantee the children will be in on the agreed day to take the call, then it's unlikely to work. Some flexibility might be OK, but you both need to be aware of it, and how you'll deal with it. For example, you might agree that their dad will call every Wednesday evening and you'll do your best to make sure they're in to take the call. Emily has found that even when friends are round, or the children are engrossed in a TV programme, they're very happy to be interrupted for a few minutes to have a quick chat with Dad. Getting them to the phone was easier than she'd anticipated. On the odd occasion when something really can't be stopped mid-flow (like a ticking-off session!), then agree that getting the children to phone back later is OK.

If you don't like the idea of being tied to a fixed day and time for a call, or it's unworkable for you or your family, being more fluid is just as good: perhaps just agreeing that Dad will phone them once a week. But it's important to understand that if he calls and you're all out, the onus is then on *you* to call back and make sure that the children do get to speak to him. He will have done his bit, so you need to do yours to make it work.

6. Creating a Schedule

Schedules are important as they help everyone to know where they stand – not just parents but children, new partners and extended family as well. They allow us to plan and to eliminate that horrible feeling of limbo and uncertainty. They mean the children know when they'll next see their dad, and that helps to reduce their angst. Knowing when you're going to be child-free can also help to keep a harassed and tired full-time single mum going!

We hope that both you and the children's dad can agree about the importance of the children seeing him and that you help each other to make it work, even if the children are reluctant. The schedules don't have to be cast in stone, just 'firm dates' that are changed not on a whim ('I fancy going to Paris for the weekend I'm due to have them; can you take them?'), but when it's practical and sensible and would be awkward if the dates weren't changed ('I've been asked to be Matron of Honour and the wedding's on one of my weekends – can we swap?').

By setting dates in advance the children know what their schedule is for the immediate future. We've found that our children like to know exactly what's happening the following weekend, when they're seeing their dad next, what they're doing during the next half-term, and that there's something to look forward to over the holidays. There's no need for them to know the schedule in detail, just the choice, finalized bits. The schedule need only then be for grown-up eyes, with an acceptance that some things may change. Manage your children's expectations by telling them when they'll next see their dad (assuming you know) and when holidays are booked.

You need to decide whether it's easier to plan for just a term at a time, or for a whole year, or whether you need to be more flexible because one of you works shifts, for example. Your child-free week-ends are important, as they'll give you a rest (and their dad should appreciate the benefits to the children of you being rested!). So how often do you need a break? And how far in advance do you need to plan to make the most of them – days, weeks, months?

Be warned, though, that scheduling time to see their dad can be a flashpoint for parents. Some dads want too much flexibility, or have got into the habit of prioritizing themselves and their own interests. This is usually because their perspective has changed or they assume that the children are fine without them for a while, or are happy and coping because their mum hasn't said otherwise.

Dear Kate and Emily,
I'm having problems with my children's father. I don't know what to do, he arranges to come over to see the children and then doesn't show up, or he cancels the day before as things have 'come up'. The children sit at the front window with their coats on waiting for him and it breaks my heart. We wait in all day for him and he never comes. Then when he does he just stays in the house and never takes them out. I find it all incredibly hard and don't know what to do, as he doesn't listen to me or stand by our arrangements.
Desperately yours,
Waiting of Wigan

Dear Waiting,
How frustrating — this sort of behaviour is upsetting for the children, and not helping you to get a break! As a first step why not explain to Dad in a positive way that the children love him and the contact he has with them is important? Try and find out from him what works best for him and therefore stands the greatest chance of being honoured. Is it after work once a week? Weekends? Saturdays? Annual leave? And so on. Explain how disappointed the children can be and then ask him to let you know as soon as he knows if he's not going to come — via text, say. You could also ask him if he wants suggestions of what to do with them,

or would he like to take on some child-related tasks like taking the children to the library, or would he like you to investigate Saturday football? If he's lacking imagination or just plain basic knowledge of how children tick, then he may welcome some ideas.

Now let's cut to the chase: as your children's father is currently unreliable it's up to you to manage their expectations. Don't tell them that their dad is due, and do something with them – playing, making things, etc. – then if he comes it'll be a nice surprise.

When he does come the contact is his responsibility. You've offered ideas, now retreat ... take yourself out if he shows up – even if it's just for a good walk. Take your book to the park, go to the flicks or window-shopping. This isn't a long-term solution, but the bit that upsets you most, we'd guess, and gets you cross, is the children's hurt. So you manage that first and then tackle him about it so you can get a proper solution.

Love, Kate and Emily

You can help to prevent time with their dad becoming a flashpoint and a problem by taking a good look at the whole year using a 52-week year planner.

Emily's year planner shows Mum's and Dad's weekends. It gets sent between them a few times starting at the beginning of each year, and each one adds in things they're thinking of doing. For example, 'It's Great-Great-Aunt Winifred's 110th birthday on June 7th and we're spending the weekend celebrating' or 'I need to go on a course in May.' Then there are dates that you know might be tricky, such as your new partner's birthday when you fancy bouncing around in a remote hut *à deux* (use tact and great diplomacy to clinch this one!). Then there are the rest of the weekends and holidays to allocate, and Christmas, New Year and other festivities to agree on. Emily also adds bank holidays, term dates, Mother's Day, Father's Day, family birthdays, friends' birthdays and other important information to provide a heads-up for things that may be happening.

This is the basis from which any changes can be negotiated over the 12-month period. Looking at a chart like this can help you both to be reasonable. It has to be used with a degree of flexibility (particularly when looking 12 months ahead; the further in advance the two of you can plan, the more fluid the agreed schedule should be). Such is the power of the Excel spreadsheet, it can be changed as situations develop. If you're not a computer whizzkid, a wall calendar, pencil and rubber combo works just as well!

If one parent is on a three-month shift rota, a 12-month plan can't be filled out completely, but chunks can, and then details can be added when rotas are known. Taking the long view like this helps both parents to realize how little or how much they're seeing the children, and to redress the balance if need be.

Finally, another reminder to *be reasonable*. For some mothers, letting their children go to stay with Dad can be very difficult. This is often because they feel over-protective and so they put up a whole string of reasons why they can't stay: 'It's too far away, they don't know your house and will be scared, they're too young, you don't have the space or the games, TV, Internet access ...' We can all think of reasons why our children shouldn't go, so the co-parenting plan challenges you to explain any restrictions you've made on when the children can see their dad (like no overnight stays). If you can't explain the restriction rationally then it's got to come out and you'll have to bite the bullet and compromise.

Dear Kate and Emily,
My husband left me a year ago and I really struggle as this is not the way I wanted to experience parenthood. I feel as though I've had part of my children's childhood taken away from me. Why should I be the one who's not with them on their birthday, or share Christmas or the holidays? Why the hell should I miss

all these lovely things when it wasn't me that left? I didn't ask
for this to happen and I really, really struggle with this bit.
Love,
Why Me of Windsor

Dear Why Me,
The short answer is: because you have to. You're in this situation and you've got to do the best for the children, and that includes letting them share high days and holidays with their dad. Planning and dividing the treats and high points need to be done in advance, and if you get it right you may realize it doesn't have to be about chopping the time down the middle. Christmas and birthdays, for example, are celebrations that CAN be shared, so think about a plan that works so that everyone gets a piece of the action. For example, Christmas is not just about December 25th, and birthdays are about more than the day too, like the party or special outing, family and cake which are all elements that can be shared around.
Let the children and their dad have good times together. Make it easy for the children to go, knowing that Mum's OK about it and happy. If you're on your own when you would rather be joining in the fun, make sure you've something planned. Distraction and diversion is the name of the game 'til they get back into your arms and then you can celebrate.
Love, Kate and Emily

7. Co-parenting Reviews

It's important for both parents to look back over the plan to see if it's working and, if not, where it can be improved in a non-confrontational way. It's also good to review the goals and objectives you set at the outset and keep focused on them. This is a key part of the co-parenting plan as it ensures that communications are kept open between the two of you.

Having these conversations is difficult, but not as difficult as trying to start them. It's easy to put off chats about the children's education or teenage problems because the time isn't right, you have to dash, you didn't get time to talk in private and so on. We've all done it. Having review meetings set in stone gets round this. Put them in the schedule and stick to them (or make a firm rearrangement if something comes up – just don't leave it open).

The frequency of the reviews will vary depending on what's going on in all of your lives. If there's nothing much on, then there's little need to review more than once or twice a year. However, if one of your common parenting issues becomes a hot news item – such as school transfers, dodgy behaviour, or uni applications – then more frequent reviews will be needed; perhaps every two months. Have a look at what's coming up over the course of the year and book reviews at sensible times with these key events in mind.

As well as enabling you to check that the plan is working and to revise it if not, these review meetings will also give you practice at talking to each other in a direct and practical way so that problems don't get blown out of proportion, or fester. You'll find it progressively easier to tell each other what's bothering you while it's still a small problem rather than a big one you've been sitting on for a while. And the very best thing that could come from these meetings might be that some of the problems won't even occur in the first place!

We've learned from our own and others' experience that you need to work hard at making sure these review meetings take place. It's very easy for them to slip because, let's face it, having such meetings isn't really anyone's idea of fun. You might feel like you've done all you can by reminding their dad about the review meeting once or twice, or saying you'll leave it up to him to name a date. But it often takes more than that and you may need to be a bit more tenacious and keep on reminding so that they don't get forgotten.

8. Complaints Procedure

> **VERY IMPORTANT NOTICE:** You'll not be able to agree on everything. Be prepared to forgo the issues you can't agree on in order to preserve those that you can. The best-laid plans of mice and separated parents can go wrong!

The complaints procedure tries to allow for a rational, calm discussion of any problems that arise. If a problem is caused by you behaving badly, remove yourself immediately from the situation and have a cooling-off period, say 48 hours, and then gingerly offer an olive branch. Then, sooner rather than later, and away from the children, get both your heads together and sort out the problem. If a decision is needed, you'll have to find a way of agreeing one. If, on the other hand, it's a hypothetical or trivial issue, leave it alone, at least for a while. Stick to co-parenting and put everything else to one side. Don't let irrelevancies, history or personal irritations muck things up, as they so easily can. Let's face it – you two have split up, so there'll be plenty of arguments waiting to happen if you choose to have them.

If you believe that things are wrong with the other person's behaviour, you need to explain your concerns when you've calmed down. Say why it upset you, how it makes you feel, and appeal to them to stop behaving like it in the future. Don't let it fester, don't speak in anger, and don't speak in haste. Then, try to stabilize the good ship *HMS Co-parent* and sail into quieter waters.

Finally ... What If He Won't Play Ball?

As you'll have gathered by now, we firmly believe that co-parenting is a worthwhile goal, but we also recognize that the reality may not always fit with the ideals we're advocating. What should you do if you're totally in favour of co-parenting, but their dad isn't, and despite your efforts at persuasion he refuses to sign up to something that to him sounds too official or too restrictive? We suggest you try to carry on as if he's in favour of it, and lead by example. Then at least you know you're doing the right thing and if he wants to ignore the situation, then so be it. However, if you can demonstrate the benefits of co-parenting through your own actions and attitude, he will hopefully reciprocate.

Dear Kate and Emily,
I'm throwing in the towel. I've had it up to here! I've done
everything by the book and he just goes and stops my money.
Bastard! Why the hell should I do anything for this pillock?!
Love,
Furious of Feltham

Dear Furious,
Why indeed? Because, pillock or not, he's the children's dad! You just have to allow him to be Dad, OK? They adore him, so let them have him, and as much of him as is possible. As for you: you don't have to have anything to do with him other than to facilitate his relationship with the children. This is your life and your new family, so start to plan it and you'll begin to feel independent.
Love, Kate and Emily

THE CO-PARENTING FORM

This form is for both you and the children's dad to read, think about and fill in. There are eight sections. You can fill it in together or do it separately and meet up to discuss your answers.

Please be honest with your answers; nothing is gained from secrecy or leaving things unsaid.

Once you've both filled it in you need to go through it together and combine those areas that you can agree on, and compromise on those that you can't.

Fix a time when you can meet to discuss what you've both written:

DATE: _____

TIME: _____

PLACE: _____

Section 1: How are you going to behave towards each other?

By writing down how you plan to behave it'll help you to achieve this even when you don't feel like it. Here is a list of types of behaviour that you could agree to. Tick the ones you know you can do, and add more that might be more relevant to your own situation.

We will try our best to:
☐ Not criticize or be disparaging about the other parent
☐ Handle all disagreements away from the children
☐ Not shout or swear
☐ Listen to one another
☐ Try to see each other's point of view
☐ Stick to what we've agreed
☐ Not deliberately antagonize each other
☐ Not play games
☐ Respect each other's personal space
☐ Try to resolve things between us
☐ Help each other to be the best parents we can

Flashpoints
Think through the subjects that you DON'T want their dad to mention.
Which parts of his life do you really NOT want to hear about?

I don't want him to mention...

_____

I don't want to hear about...

_____

Section 2: Your parenting objectives
Write down your objectives as a parent – in both the long term and over the coming year.

My long-term parenting objectives are:

_____

My parenting objectives for the year are:

_____

Section 3: Parenting areas to discuss with each other
Make your own list of areas that you would like to discuss with their dad. Areas you'd like to share your views on, and to find out his.

1 _____
2 _____
3 _____
4 _____
5 _____
6 _____

Getting Support to Help Achieve Your Parenting Objectives
Look back at your own parenting objectives for the year. Can any of these be achieved better if you co-parent? How can their dad help achieve any part of these?

Section 4: Communicating with their dad

Tick what you feel is the **most effective** way for you to communicate with their dad about each of these subjects.

The most effective one will be where you are **both** able to speak, and you are **both** able to make yourselves understood.

Subject to discuss	Text	Email	Phone	Face to face	Third party (relative or friend)
Day-to-day stuff about the children					
Concerns about the children					
Long-term plans for the children (e.g. schools, college, leaving home)					
Sorting out holidays					
Logistics of Dad seeing the children					
Changing plans					
You – what your plans are, new partners, new job, etc					
Their dad – what his plans are, new partners, new job, etc					

What other things come up for discussion between you? How do you want to communicate about these?

Other subjects to discuss	Text	Email	Phone	Face to face	Third party (relative or friend)

Section 5: Keeping Dad in touch with the children

How would you like their dad to keep in touch with the children? Think through the following:

- What would be the best way of keeping in touch with them (phone, email, text, staying at his place)?
- Any particular time of day?
- Any particular day of the week?
- Is it better as regular or irregular contact?

Dad keeping in touch at:	How? Any particular day? Planned or unplanned?
Weekends	
Weekdays	
Holidays	

Any exceptions or times when you *don't* want contact?

Is there anything that makes keeping regular contact difficult, or that makes scheduling contact difficult? Why?

_____

_____

_____

Section 6: Creating a schedule

Think about the schedule for the children's time at their dad's home. When you're discussing the schedule is it easier to plan for just a term at a time, for a whole year, or to be more flexible?

I'd like to plan the weekend *schedule:* _____*in advance*

What about planning holidays: how much in advance would you like these to finalized?

I'd like to plan the holiday *schedule:* _____*in advance*
Is there anything else to note about agreeing these schedules?

_____

_____

_____

Now do the same for **changing arrangements**. When do you need to know by? How flexible can you be? Why?

_____

_____

_____

High Days and Holidays
How would you like to divide the bank holidays, Easter and Christmas holidays between you?

Holidays	How to share them
Bank Holidays	
Easter	
Christmas	
New Year	

Section 7: Co-parenting reviews
What would you put on the agenda? Would you put any of these on your agenda?

☐ Education   ☐ Sports/hobbies
☐ Achievements   ☐ Behaviour
☐ Medical   ☐ Extended family
☐ Anything on the horizon? Exams, holidays, sports fixtures, etc.?

☐ Share parenting tips of things that you've found worked (or didn't) with the children

What else would you put on your list?

1 _____

2 _____

3 _____

How frequently would you like to meet up to discuss the children and go through this agenda?

☐ Once every three months/every term
☐ Once every six months
☐ Once a year
☐ Something else?

Where would you like to have this meeting? In your house, their house, out somewhere? Over a coffee, a drink, a meal? Why's that the best venue?

_____

_____

_____

Section 8: Complaints procedure

There will always be a time when things will go wrong between you. The trick is to get back on track ASAP.

If their dad had a complaint to make about you, or something was bugging him, how would you like to hear about it? How would you like him to deal with it?

_____

_____

_____

_____

Can you see yourself being able to manage complaints or irritations you've got with their dad like this?

☐ Yes
☐ No

If '**no**', then you need to change what your expectations of him are, so that they match the way you're able to behave.

Dear Kate and Emily,

I've been separated now for a little more than a year, after 20 years of marriage and two children (ten and nine). I told my husband to leave after discovering he was having an affair. We had always lived between Edinburgh and Portsmouth, and because the children go to school in Scotland and I work there, I decided after the separation to stay there.

My ex works and lives in Portsmouth, so he's keen to stay in the house when he comes to see the children. I work full time, take care of my children full time and when he does come to spend time with them he's camped out on my sofa! He chooses his dates of arrival and pretends in front of the children that we're one happy family. Sometimes I go and stay with friends when he's there but mostly I hide in a B&B. I don't think this is normal and if you know of others in the same situation I would love to know how they handle this. I'm trying to move on but I feel that he's refusing to let me! Any suggestions?

Thanks,

Hiding in Hotels of Edinburgh

Dear Hiding in Hotels,

We think that the arrangement that you have is on the unusual side. Kate does this type of thing (ex coming over to stay in their house so he can see the children) but it works for them.

The part of your arrangement that we couldn't handle (and so we'd suggest you change it) is the lack of discussion and planning about the time when your ex is 'on duty'.

Why not sit down with him and plan the year? Or if you can't do that, a six-month period of time? Explain to him that if this arrangement is to carry on you need to be able to plan and use the time to recharge your batteries and that the children need to know when he's coming etc., etc. There has got to be some give and take here.

Then, once you know when you've got free time, use the time for YOU. Don't hide in hotels, do the MoT section (see pages 40-44) and think about taking up new interests, make for the mountains, do charity work, catch up on work, whatever ... Make the time count because it's so important and, let's face it, you can do this as you know your children are happy in their own home.

The other thing you say is that your ex is pretending you're a happy family. Hopefully the children will be clear that this arrangement doesn't mean that Mum and Dad are getting back together. Try to reinforce that. In the meantime, go with the good vibe. It's not a good idea to remind him constantly in front of the children that you've not forgotten, nor forgiven; that would merely create one of those horrible atmospheres which, to be frank, is very bad for the children, horrific for you, and totally unacceptable in your own home.

So if you can manage it, make him plan a proper schedule of time with the children and use the time when he's at the helm wisely. If you can't manage this arrangement, think carefully about alternatives. Do you really want the children making a very long journey on a regular basis, or your ex taking your children to a hotel in Edinburgh? See if you can think of anything that would be better for all of you. If you think about the pros and cons of the alternatives, this might make you realize that him coming to the children is not so bad after all.

Love, Kate and Emily

Dear Kate and Emily,

My partner and I separated six months ago. We have a 2½-year-old little girl. We're on good speaking terms and are both set on being as involved in her upbringing as possible. We really want to share the parenting fairly and productively. So far, our little one spends one week at Daddy's, one week at Mummy's and so on. She seems OK with this, and we meet up once all together at the weekends. But a week must seem very long to her and we both sense a distance from her when the 'next' parent takes her home at the start of the week. For her dad and me as well, it feels a bit draining and confusing being a single parent one week, and a single child-free adult the next. We think it would be better if she spent a shorter block of time with each of us: 4 days, for example, seems more balanced, less extreme. However, it's not obvious how it's possible to alternate weekday care and weekends while having a routine that is sustainable and cyclical. Can you recommend a fairer and more fluid way of dividing up the time? Many thanks!

Love,

Want to be Fair of Fairfax

Dear Want to be Fair,

Firstly, well done on sharing your parenting so well and clearly being able to discuss the pros and cons with your daughter's father. It's this very fact which means we're going to seem to duck the issue and say that only talking about the pros and cons in detail between you and looking at them from the point of view of all three of you will help make the solution more clear. You see, we don't think there's a perfect solution. The very fact that you and your ex are bringing up your daughter apart means that the situation is less than ideal from a shared parenting point of view, so any solution will be a compromise — which one you choose is down to you three. We remember listening to a child and family expert saying once that children can alternate homes happily, as long as they have all they need, their 'stuff' is in each home, and that both homes are near school, friends, etc. so their life outside the home remains constant. We also don't think that the reconnection issue will be any better after four days than after seven — just more frequent. Our gut feeling is that the distanced feeling when she first comes home is a function of being brought up in this way — but it's probably a worthwhile downside when it's weighed up against the fact that both her parents are equally involved, she sees both equally, and will grow up seeing you both on good terms, etc. Sorry — a long way of saying that we think you're probably doing the best you can and that all you need to do really is decide if the downside of a week on/week off is more or less than the downside of any other arrangement, as they will ALL have downsides for ALL of you!

Love, Kate and Emily

" Divorce is not rocket science. You observe the marriage is not working. You file for divorce. The divorce comes through. You realise the crucial thing is to protect your children and to put your own selfish instincts on hold. You understand, because you've two brain cells to rub together, that since stopping being married doesn't mean stopping being parents, this involves creating another kind of relationship with the children's father/mother. You do this, everyone is a bit shaken up and gets on with it and becomes happy. The end. "
India Knight, *The Times*

" I began to realise that divorce need not be the catastrophic failure and shameful end of everything that I had feared. Somewhere at the bottom of my gloom I saw how life went on, rearranged and restructured, and that children need love more than they need legal contracts and orthodox patterns of behaviour. "
Joan Bakewell, *The Centre of the Bed: An Autobiography* Sceptre

Chapter 6

REINVENTING YOUR FAMILY

Families, nuclear and extended, can be the most wonderful of things, offering unconditional love and a support system second to none. But when they go wrong, whey hey, enormous amounts of chaos, distress and fallout can ensue.

What you hope and want for your family will be shaped by your own experiences and observations, and these will develop into quite firm dreams and expectations. Maybe as a child you had a carefree, secure and wonderful childhood and want your children to have the same experience? Or perhaps you had a less happy time, the consequence of which is that you have a crystal-clear picture of how you *don't* want your children to experience family? One thing is for sure, it's unlikely that the shape of the family you have now is the one you set out to achieve. So now what?

Your mindset needs reprogramming slightly to accommodate the fact that you're no longer with your children's father. Rest assured, your nuclear family is still very much there and can be every bit as good as a traditional Mum-and-Dad set up.

However it will be different, and in order to get the most out of your new team and create a real sense of family it does need a little bit of thinking about, hatching and planning.

First things first: every team needs a manager, and although there are lots of lovely things you can do to help shape this new squad, do remember that YOU need to stay in charge. As the parent you still need to maintain boundaries, rules and discipline. Hard and exhausting but you know it makes sense! Obviously you don't want to be the bad guy all the time, and in the long run you won't be, but meantime you've a tricky balancing act between tough love and the more coodgy side of parenting. Try not to let the children milk the situation too much! That may seem harsh when they've already been through a lot, but being too spoily and over-indulgent makes things harder for you. You run the risk of losing control, which would be a nightmare. We all know that from the age of dot to late teens children like to know what's what, what they can do and what they can't, what's expected of them and what's unacceptable – it makes rebelling so much easier!

Yes, you may need to find a new parenting style, but it must be one where you're the leader of the pack.

Stop right there and think for a minute of all the families (real, fictional, historical and current) that work without the traditional Mum-and-Dad scenario and you'll realize that you too can have a great, strong, positive unit full of love, fun, caring and warmth that will send fuzzy shivers down your spine.

Here are some of our favourites:

- *Anne of Green Gables* (Anne adopted as an orphan by a couple of old folk)
- HRH Prince Andrew and Fergie (always seem to be laughing like drains)
- Bob Geldof (he's made a marvellous fist of what might appear to be an unusually shaped family).

No, we don't know what really goes on in these families, but then you don't in any family. Looking at, and thinking about, what appears to be a good set up can at least get you thinking in a positive way about the whole 'different family' thing.

As Kate often says, 'Same frame, different photograph,' or as Emily says (as two can play the daft cliché game), 'Same tank, different fish.' It just takes a bit of effort. Begin by concentrating on what you and your children *have* got, rather than hanging on to the images of what you used to have.

Read these points several times and digest them fully:

- Your family still exists, it's just a slightly different shape.
- The family you thought you would have has changed.
- You don't know what's going on in other people's families, so stop looking longingly at the regular shapes and see where people are having a great time in the less conventional set ups.
- It's highly likely that there are things in your past life that you're better off without, just as there are things in your new life to celebrate.
- Don't try to be brave by putting yourself in painful situations. Be realistic about what will upset you and if you think something will make you feel uncomfortable, avoid it.
- Learn to count what you've got, not what you've lost. Know that longing for what you don't have can spoil all the goodness from what you've got.
- Do everything in your power to make friends with a family that is also asymmetrical.

'I'm the Leader, I'm the Leader, I'm the Leader of the Gang I Am!'

We can't pretend that it's always easier with one parent; it often isn't and one of the trickiest departments is discipline. Even though your family is a new and different shape it still needs someone at the helm, and as you're in charge it's worth thinking long and hard about law and order. Kate is from a big, noisy family of loud and forthright women, so you might have thought that she's never had a problem controlling her own ship ... nothing could be further from the truth! Emily's found discipline and the need to stick to the rules among the most exhausting and depressing aspects of life as a single parent, so she's fixed on her end-goals of sending the children out into the big, wide world well-enough equipped to make friends and not pee them off, to stay out of trouble with the law, to charm elderly relatives and anyone in authority, and to sit still in restaurants. The rest is 'nice to haves', but the discipline and house rules are all focused on her end-goals.

Here's a medley of tips that we've discovered through trial and error work for us when driving and manoeuvring that vehicle that is 'the family'.

Top Tips

- Kate reckons that picking your battles is the way forward, as she'd make herself hoarse, and send the neighbours running for cover, if she were to shout and tell her children off ALL the time. The trouble is that a good telling-off can wreck the whole atmosphere of the family for the evening or weekend, particularly when there's no other adult you can have a laugh with or who can defuse the situation, or whom you can just ask to take over when you've had enough. So go ape only when it's really called for.
- Work out a punishment scale for misdemeanours, make sure everyone knows, understands, and agrees to it, and then STICK to it. It's hard – and in fact Kate did only stick to the 'no scooters to school' punishment because she knew her neighbour had witnessed the sordid family meltdown and heard the punishment being handed out, and would be out cleaning the brasses the next morning. To scoot past would've been just too embarrassing and weak!
- This one's a biggy of a top tip: carry it through. Don't threaten punishments you don't want, or can't carry through (e.g. 'We won't go to Granny's this weekend' – you're going whatever happens!).

- We're both relaxed about friends and family pulling the children into line. This is quite a tricky one as it can make you feel a bit hopeless, so get into the positive way of thinking about encouraging your nearest and dearest to help you. Let them know that you'll not think of it as a criticism of your parenting skills, but as help. Just as loving family members did in the past when Mum had a brood of 14. This is only telling-off territory where safety, unkindness and unacceptable behaviour of a minor misdemeanour are involved, not complete and utter 'ballistic rocketing' serious stuff (that's our job!).
- If you see your child being naughty and his behaviour can't be accepted, not serious but at the same time not condonable, which is about 60% of incidents (data based on pure guesswork), rather than scream and shout, sometimes just pretend you haven't seen it or noticed it.
- Try to raise the children's participation in the family. The family meeting is great for encouraging the children to learn and accept that there's a right way to behave which makes life easier for everyone.
- Work with the school if behaviour is becoming a problem.
- Talk to the children and talk to their dad to see if there is an underlying worry or concern that is making them behave badly. Maybe they need a little bit of undivided 1-2-1 attention with you or their dad. Bake a cake together, icing and all.
- Emily finds that consistency and not giving in are most of the 'battle' won, as the children throw in the towel just before she's about to! They get the hang of the rules and then the nagging decreases, though obviously never goes away totally. And you get to repeat yourself less often and to spend more time having pleasant conversations rather than stand-offs.
- Share out some of the smaller responsibilities and chores. This gives all family members the feeling that you're a team that they have a stake in.

How Kate and Emily Reinvented Their Families

Kate and her gang

The third of four sisters, I'm not used to being alone – so when I was first on my own I felt like a real fish out of water. The children were very small and to stop going bonkers I'd rotate around my friends and family pretty much every weekend. We rarely stayed at home for the first year. Then I realized that I had to stop touring the country. Visiting had become exhausting for everyone: packing the car, travelling, and constantly bolting on to other people's families. My sisters' and friends' poor husbands would see me roaring over the hill with travel cots and all manner strewn over the back of my beaten-up estate car, and as I was poured out of the vehicle, my children sorted, and I was handed a drink, the poor husband could be seen making for the potting shed sharpish!

All jesting aside, as lovely and welcoming as my friends and family were, it was time for me to move on. I felt that this couldn't go on forever and we needed to be in our own home and to find ways to be content without other people. We needed to create a community nearer to home. I started our own little routines and rituals, partly to create some structure to the weekends so I wasn't thinking 'What shall we do now?' and spiralling into decline. These rituals have changed and evolved as the children have grown but some things have stayed the same and are totally part of our family life now. As you'll notice from our rituals below, they're based around what I like doing! Not being the selfless type I haven't made myself go and sit in an indoor soft play area every Sunday afternoon! I was very undemocratic about the whole procedure at the outset and decided what we were up to, and told them. I should add they were very small at the time and this bulldozer technique may not work as well with older children! But for me there was no asking what they thought, wanted to do, etc. That could've led to arguments and tears when there was no need.

Kate's family rituals

- I like coffee, so every Saturday without the routine of school we get up and go and have breakfast out. We've done local cafés, picnics in the park, Starbucks, McDonalds, Little Chefs. The principle is to get the weekend going, get decent coffee, the children fed and to avoid washing up.
- Bed-sharing stopped but was replaced by morning cuddles. Sunday morning is all into my bed at 7 a.m. with a Disney film on. I go back to sleep while the children watch the film cuddled up to their very own 'sleeping beauty'.
- I decided to start going to church as the Sunday School was great for the children and I got 40 minutes' 'space' to think in a bit of peace.
- I cook a roast every Sunday and we often invite other people over to eat with us. It might be a single parent with children, or it might not be. Afterwards we go walking and gather cones, sticks and leaves, or else we make a mess with the craft stuff in the kitchen.
- Once a year we go away, just the three of us, for a walking holiday to the Lakes.
- We often have Saturday lunch with Dad. This is a great success as I don't cook and we play word games and card games over a pizza.
- As the children have got older I try to match task with treats, though keeping pocket money separate – I don't want them to think they're being paid to help.
- Periodically we sit down over a meal and write a list of things we'd all like to do soon: go strawberry-picking, go to the science museum, visit Fran, make a chocolate angel cake and so on, and then we work through them over the next month or so.
- We all have a patch of the garden to tend, which we enjoy. (Emily says it makes my garden look like an old folks' home, lots of different garish colours mingled in with veg!)

These are things I've done over the last seven years, not all at the same time. I started some things that petered out and some that have really taken off. But I do try to focus them around simple inexpensive fun that's pretty much centred around us being together. We do spend a lot of our spare time together at home, and you may have noticed that a lot of it is based around food!

Emily and her gang

It's hard to remember back now, but I think the children and I have always been pretty much home-based. In the early days we definitely were, as I really wasn't in the mood for a tour of friends, worried that I'd have to justify why I'd left my husband. On my child-free weekends I'd take myself off to see my family and oldest and closest friends for a bit of distraction, company, being cared for, and a change of scene. But with the children we stayed put and slowly began to get used to being a threesome. My mum and dad are local, so often we'd go to them for a day so that the children would be happily entertained by active and doting grandparents and I'd get looked after and have adult company too. It was time, really, that helped to make it feel normal to us. The more you spend time together, the quicker you feel like a little unit again. One of the nice sides of being a single parent is that, because there's only one of you, you can't divide and conquer – if one goes, you all go, so my children are very good friends as they spend so much time together, and we feel like a very close family where we all look out for each other.

It took a while to get to this stage, though, but doing some of this lot helped:

- I changed the house a bit, nothing too dramatic but I made it look and feel different, reinforcing the fact we were a new family. I let the children have a say in the house to help make them feel like it was ours rather than just mine. As a result we've had the TV move position on numerous occasions, tables and chairs repositioned, and now they want to paint their rooms!
- We got a rabbit and a guinea pig (who would be very fed up if I didn't name-check them – big shout to Twix and Sausage), which has

really helped to make us feel like a fully functioning 'normal' family!

- Harmony between me and the children is what makes our family work, so when it goes wrong I make a concerted effort to give the three of us my attention and bind us together again by stopping doing my chores and then counting to 10 extremely slowly and, when I've calmed down (or they've clamed down), I concentrate just on us and making sure that whoever was wobbly feels safe, loved and part of the family again. And if I was the wobbly one, then I've still got my mummy!

- 'Grown-up time' is a weekend night when the children join in my adult time and can stay up a bit late, talk to any adult guests, eat crisps and have a drink.

- Video nights – all of us out to choose a film and then back to the sofa to watch.

- We eat together every evening unless I'm going out, and sometimes they help cook or choose the menu.

- Annual camping trip to the New Forest for a weekend. I can do no more than three nights max!

- A trip to the panto, outdoor ice skating and flashing lights all over the house have become our own Christmas traditions.

Dear Kate and Emily,

I'm 38 years old and became a single mum about 14 months ago, and I'm really struggling to come to terms with what's happened. I keep comparing myself to all the parents my age who seem to be married and whose children are being brought up in an environment I wanted to bring my daughter up in. I'm so jealous and sad that it hasn't worked out that way for my daughter.

Please can you help with any advice on how to move forward?

Love,

Can't Stop Comparing of Cardiff

Dear Can't Stop Comparing,

We know what you mean — we too find Christmas, Valentine's Day, etc. very hard for the same reason — it's amazing that as soon as you don't have a husband or boyfriend by your side EVERYONE else seems to! And they're all handsome AND incredibly attentive AND not at all shy of public displays of affection — it feels very unfair! However, in all seriousness, we also know that behind many a door is an unhappy marriage, with one or other of them looking at YOU and thinking how lucky YOU are to be able to live on your own, have the TV remote all to yourself, cook and eat when and what you like, set your own house rules, have no one to argue with or irritate you at the end of a busy day, say yes or no to invitations or ideas without having to ask your husband first, be able to grow the hairs on your legs as long as you want, go out on the town and do things that married people miss, like meeting new people, bar-hopping, etc. Many married people see not only the advantages of being single, but also the opportunities that being single can bring. Many of them will be looking at you from within a marriage that they feel has stopped them from doing things they'd love to do — like an evening course, taking up a hobby like photography, turning half of the living room into some-where they could write the book they've always dreamed of, or paint or make jewellery, go back to work and be a 'grown-up' again, etc.

You see, an upside of being single is that all of a sudden you're in complete charge of your own life — no one else other than your daughter to consider, so you can start to explore things you haven't before. It's called making the best of a bad situation in order to turn it into a better one, and then eventually into a good one! So what did we do? Well, Emily did an evening sewing course at the local college and made some brown gingham pyjamas that have since fallen apart (doesn't sound much, but sewing clothes is something she'd always wanted to be able to do — clearly still more work to do on that front!), and then she said 'Yes' to Kate when she asked her to do something called 'Kate and Emily' with her! She'd never have said that if she'd still been married, as she'd have worried about being selfish spending all that time doing something that she wanted to do rather than something that would benefit her husband too. And Kate made some new friends who were single mums whose company she enjoyed, so she had a laugh with them and could meet up with them in the pub. We're not suggesting you meet millions of new people — but even one or two makes a difference.

So where's all this going ...? Well, it's only been 14 months, it'll take time to stop noticing all those apparently happy families quite so much, but what helps is doing things that make your new life FEEL like a new life. Use the parents you know at school to find other single mums and dads, and ask them if they fancy going to the pub one night, and then book it (we don't know one single parent who'd turn down the offer of company and an evening out, so don't be shy!). Be open to opportunity by keeping an open mind, positive outlook and happy face, and adventures, big or small, will find you — perhaps you could make a pair of pyjamas that last for more than three months?!

This has been a very rambling reply, but buried in there somewhere are the things that we did to make life feel positive rather than a failure.

Good luck, Kate and Emily

When the Children Won't Play Ball

It must be hard if your children are very angry and upset that their old family has gone. Maybe they have had to move home and really don't want to get involved in any of the 'getting on with it' type of ideas we've got. If this is the case, then we'd urge you to keep going in a clear, consistent and gentle way:

- Cook as many meals as you can for the family to eat together. This applies to everyone, as eating round a table is the single most effective thing you can do to glue your family together. Great if it can be breakfast, lunch or supper, but even if it's a cup of hot choc and a bun before bed, or a cup of tea in the morning, it can be a great leap forward. If meals start around the table in silence or dissolve into arguments, still stick at them, as conversations will arise and you'll begin to get a sense of all looking out for each other and listening to everyone's tales of the day.
- Try and play games together. Cards, Scrabble, Consequences – whatever you think the children might like, and will all be able to join in with. Think of the games you used to enjoy. Pen-and-paper games and Rummikub are a great success *chez* Kate, and card games the best with that old shark Emily.
- Find something on the TV to watch together with a bowl of pop-corn. It's very easy to regress into children's TV, or else try *The Simpsons*, re-runs of *Dad's Army* or *Happy Days* – the types of things that appeal to many different age groups.
- While in a period of re-grouping, just try to BE together without any pressure to be jolly.

Family Meetings

The funny thing about family meetings is that although they sound ghastly, they really can get the gang communicating better, talking and listening and helping to problem-solve. So surely it has to be worth a go?

The very concept of a meeting smacks of the workplace and it may seem very odd to use a communication idea more closely associated with the boardroom than the family. But any team, domestic or corporate, will work better if the members have effective ways of communicating, so there's no reason why families shouldn't have meetings.

All too often, conversations with the children are snatched on the way in or out of the door. As children get older their diaries compete with ours (and usually win!) and time to talk as a family can be scarce.

However, these get-togethers aren't just suitable for older children. Start early, as children as young as three can understand and become involved. Having family meetings is a really excellent way of getting your children used to the idea of teamwork, which is useful when it comes to delegating some of your housework chores while getting them used to the concept of 'not letting the side down', which can be a boon for assisting behaviour management. Family meetings can also be the ideal forum to plan weekends and holidays and to talk about manners, conduct and house rules.

So, if you fancy hosting a family meeting, follow this very simple plan:

1. Tell the children that you'll be holding a meeting in the kitchen serving popcorn, fizzy drinks, cakes, etc. in half an hour.
2. Tell them that you would like to start having regular times when you can talk about specific things. Keep the list positive and constructive (such as holidays, upcoming birthdays, etc.), but do include some more contentious topics, such as pocket money and chores. Then ask the children for other (sensible!) ideas.
3. Set some rules, such as only the person holding the teddy bear/carrot, etc. can speak. Make sure everyone has a chance to participate by passing round the teddy bear/carrot. TV and telephones stay off or unanswered.
4. You could also come up with a family name for these meetings.
5. Schedule more family meetings. For example, set the next one for next Friday at 6.30 and put a list up on the fridge with things to talk about. Encourage the others to add to it.

Top tips for family meetings
- You need to try to do more than just chair the meeting: share ideas, think aloud, and ask for solutions to problems that the children might be able to help you with. *How can I sort the cellar out? What shall I get Aunty Helen for her birthday?* Etc.

- Rotate the person who's chairing each meeting. Initially this is likely to be you, but once your children have got the idea, they too can take on this role. Family meetings always work best when the adults participate, discuss and problem-solve, rather than just referee.
- Remember that the first meeting is likely to be, at best, awkward. But don't let that put you off.
- Reinforce the importance of joining in and how much you value their input; your children will appreciate an opportunity to express how they feel in a constructive setting. It takes a while to get into the groove – patiently give the children an opportunity to express themselves in a calm environment.
- Meetings can be ad-hoc or regular: whatever suits your family. But really they should be held as often as is comfortable and necessary.
- Stay with the real issues and don't get sidetracked. Keep the meetings short and stick to an agenda. Focus on each other's strengths, not weaknesses, and remember to plan for fun.
- If you've had 'one of those days' and it has all gone wrong and you, or one of the children, just don't feel like a constructive discussion, postpone it until tomorrow. It's important that the adults at least are taking part in a calm and positive frame of mind!
- Make sure everyone has a piece of paper and a pencil. Keep a record of the family meeting and keep it for future reference.
- Make sure everyone agrees action points, and set a date and time for the next meeting.

Some potential pitfalls

First, trying to find a time that works for everyone can be difficult. If someone simply can't make it, ask them for their views on the things you were planning on discussing. Then let them know afterwards what happened and what decisions were made.

Another potential pitfall is when children (especially older ones) act as if having a family meeting is stupid or childish. Rather than drag them to the meeting, let them know they don't have to come but that some important things are going to be discussed that they may be involved in, such as who will get what chores, or where the family will go on their holiday. That should ensure their involvement – who wants to be put on 'changing beds' without having had the opportunity to fight it?!

Suggested ideas for the agenda

Our ideas may not be yours, but depending on budget, taste, and the ages of your children, do try and find some things to keep the agenda lively:

- What about a 'no TV' night when we play games instead?
- Let's plan one outdoor activity a month to do together.
- What shall we do about the garden? Dig a pond, let it go wild, plant out garden pots from plants or seeds?
- Who wants to invite some friends over? Shall we have a party?
- Anyone want to join the library and go once a month?
- Shall we get a new pet? (Only if you want one!)
- Let's think of good things to do on the next bank holiday, or to celebrate Mummy's birthday ...

Try and let your hair down, dare to do something different, look out for things to do together, try and spend some time with each child separately and try to laugh, relax and have fun together. And don't be ground down by the 'Dunno, don't care, whatever' type of talk! If that happens, stop asking the questions. Take the lead and tell them. All this family-focused stuff will really help to form your new family!

High Days and Holidays

Looking back on our own childhoods, many memories are often focused around high days and holidays. The traditions that you as a family have can strengthen and bind (even the shocking ones like the annual 400-mile journey to The Lakes on minor roads, or dear old

Aunty Gwen's hysterically unusable Christmas presents, or Granny's inedible pastry).

Even though Mum and Dad aren't together, there are ways that you can ensure that children's holidays and special days are remembered for what they are, rather than for what they're not. This may sound a tall order, but remember that this is not about splashing a load of money around, but having fun in new ways. If you can carry on some traditions, great, but in addition you need to start developing some new ones.

It's not all going to be like *The Waltons*. There'll be times that make you wonder why you bother, but when you do something and it really works and you all end up enjoying a fab day (maybe it was a picnic and game of football in the park or a day making things out of old cardboard boxes), then you'll realize that it's worth it. When you hit a winner, make a mental note to repeat the day next year (or sooner) and, hey presto! you're starting your own new family traditions and the year becomes punctuated by things to look forward to.

Grandparents

Grandparents, if your children are lucky enough to have any, can be truly FABULOUS. Another set of people to love, support and guide them, they can contribute hugely to children's sense of belonging, history and roots while providing a different perspective and take on life. To top it all they love your children warts and all and they're impossible to bore about the children. Into the bargain a good relationship with the older generation teaches all manner of lessons about the value of senior citizens, how to look after older family members and so on. It's easy to see the benefits from the children's perspective, but what about you? Maybe you don't find them easy and being with them is hard work. Perhaps you've had 'words' or just know they never liked you or are critical of the way you do things and are now really putting the boot in? Even though you know that they saw all this coming and are itching to say, 'I told you so, you sent him into the arms of another because you didn't clean the brass properly!' this isn't really the point as they can be very good for you and your children. So try and realistically put yourself into their Hush Puppies and help them to do the best they can!

A young teenager whose parents have divorced told us that her grandparents are almost more important to her than her parents are at the moment because, while her parents are wrapped up in their break-up, their own distress and their own lives, her grandparents are looking out for her and know she needs them to be there for her. So she visits them and talks to them and they give her stability and unconditional love in a tricky time. Hopefully her parents will be back on track soon and be able to focus on her again, but until that day her grandparents are doing a very good job.

This story helps to illustrate just how important grandparents can be during the aftermath of separation and divorce. It's useful if everyone realizes that grandparents can make a difference, and play an important and useful supporting role by contributing to the children's sense of belonging as well as providing a good relationship which can stand the children in good stead in the future.

But ...

Make no mistake, the relationship between the adults of both generations and sides of a break-up is often incredibly fragile and pretty easy to destabilize. So this situation needs a lot of effort and gentle handling. It's up to all the adults involved to realize that it would be a real, real shame if the grandparents dropped out of the picture. The harsh truth is that if the relationship with grandparents becomes toxic or a conflict zone, if they stoke the fire and fan the flames or if they feel the hurt of their child so keenly that they take it upon themselves to get involved in the battle, then they are jeopardizing their relationship with their child and with their grandchildren.

If at all possible, do try and involve the seniors in the process that is co-operative co-parenting so that they understand something which may be radical and unnatural to them. Show them the co-parenting plan (or at least tell them about it) and explain to them why this is the way you and your ex are going to carry on and that you're going to try to bring the children up in as civil and 'together' a way as possible. This could well be revolutionary stuff to them, as they're not used to folk carrying on like this. For them divorce may well mean line in the sand, daggers drawn, let battle commence.

That said, once they get over any awkwardness they may feel, and see that this is good for the children and that they can be involved, then they'll get with the rhythm surprisingly quickly.

Top tips to help encourage grandparents

- Let them know how important they are to the children (and you).
- Ask them how they'd like to be involved, and on what basis. Sometimes grandparents are worried about being seen to be too interfering and don't like to offer help in case it causes offence. You raising the subject and encouraging them to be involved overcomes these concerns.
- Encourage and organize the children to write postcards from holidays, send birthday cards, and ring them up when they want to share some news. Just like any other relationship, it has to be a two-way street. Thank-you cards, etc. will go a long way.

Dos and Don'ts for Grandparents

- Never go against the parents' wishes, assuming they won't find out.
- Don't get involved, criticize parenting techniques or badmouth either parent.
- Stay in regular and constant touch with phone calls, cards, letters, email.
- Establish rules and offer help, childcare, babysitting, holidays, homework – and stick to arrangements.
- Establish some little rituals with the children. Play card or board games, teach them to cook or sew, get them involved in your interests and show them interesting, quirky nicknacks and bits and pieces from yesteryear.

- Talk about your parents, your childhood and tell the children about their parent's lives as children. Show them photos, old school reports, anything you have.
- If you want to start again after a period of acrimony, well and truly wipe the slate clean and work with both parents. Read the co-parenting chapter of this book and see if you can get any tips.

Kate's Perspective

I suspected at the outset that if I left it completely up to their dad, then the children might not see much of his parents, so in the early days they were on my list of homes to visit and always made me feel welcome. When I visit, my ex-mother-in-law plays with and entertains the children while I get a break, and then as she's an amazing cook she feeds us all wonderful food. It's great for the children and they have a lovely relationship with that part of the family. We don't delve around in 'what happened' as their son will always be their son, so it would be silly and counter-productive to prod that one. They've turned into a couple of friends; my ex-mother-in-law talks about as much as I do, so we both rabbit on while my father-in-law (a farmer) will let me know when he thinks I've put on a bit too much weight in that way that some farmers do! He then takes my boy out on the land, leaving my girl to poke about in Granny's make-up. The children speak to the grandparents on the phone regularly, send postcards and share news with them. The ex-in-laws send cards from wherever they're on holiday and to mark high days and holidays. They always make a special fuss of birthdays, even if it's not on the actual day. If I need help with the children they come to stay. The children feel as much a part of that side of the family as if I had stayed married to their son. They never criticize what I do with the children and praise them to the hilt. They talk a lot about the past and get out Dad's old toys to play with, delve around the photo albums and talk about all the other members of the family, which the children love.

Emily's Perspective

Emily divides and conquers a bit with the children's dad. He makes sure the children see his parents fairly regularly and that they speak to them on the phone, send birthday cards, presents and thank-you letters. Emily likes this arrangement because she has a memory like a sieve so her ex-in-laws' birthdays always slip her mind, and her weekends with the children are infrequent enough for her to want to spend them doing things with her own side of family. It means the children get to see their other grandparents when they're with Dad at weekends or for holidays, and have a very good sense of belonging to both sides of their family. Emily's parents have been perfect examples of modern-day grandparents, sending their ex-son-in-law birthday cards, Christmas cards, and chatting with him as Emily's mum hands over the children to him on 'his' Fridays. Emily's mum and dad always talk positively to the children about their dad. It has helped to normalize an abnormal situation for everyone, including them, as they too were of course upset about the divorce. Emily believes they have played a pivotal role in helping everyone learn how to get on in a perfectly civil way again, at a time when you're not sure how you should behave.

Dear Kate and Emily,

I've just separated from my husband. We were married for six years. I've always got on well with my mum and dad, especially since having children of my own. But it's all very odd now and I'm resenting them as they've begun interfering and always phoning up or popping round and telling me what they think about the children's behaviour, or the state of the house, or making comments about my boyfriend. It's ridiculous. When I was married they'd never dare make such comments and now it's open season and it's like I'm a useless little girl again. I'm

thinking of moving to another area to get them off my back.
My mum and I've already had a falling out. Why are they being
so interfering and treating me like a child?
Love,
Daughter Again of Dundee

Dear Daughter Again,
All we can say is that we recognize this very peculiar feeling of regressing from adult to child. As married women we made all sorts of decisions about things which parents never ever dared comment on! And then your marriage ends and your parents go from backseat observers to backseat drivers, and it's because they're parents and love us — just as we love our own children. Our crisis brings their parent-love and protective streak to the fore. We recommend that you recognize why you're falling out with your parents (you're not used to being mothered and they're being overly protective). Then you need to tell them how odd it feels, and why you might be snappy or defensive with them. And then they can appreciate the fine line between support and interference that they must tread. We can only reassure you that if you keep calm and don't over-react, this feeling of being cared about and being looked after will become rather nice! Don't forget that they're as interested in you and your children as you are, and make a great sounding-board, as well as giving emotional and/or practical support. So, Daughter Again, stay in Dundee and tell your mum why you've been tetchy, give each other a little leeway and look forward to a great relationship with people who can be your best support and biggest fans!
Love, Kate and Emily

The Importance of Extending Your Gang

So your immediate nuclear family has shrunk – be warned, it does mean you and the children will feel like a poor excuse for a family for a while. Perhaps the most important way of helping you all feel part of a family again is to build an extension. We're talking brothers, sisters, uncles, aunts, cousins and grandparents, and any great-great relatives you can find. We're also going beyond blood to those people who have become regular, constant and good people to have in your lives, as well as those you think could be great role models and mentors for your children. If your children have godparents or were given sponsors when they were born, then bring them up to the front row! Start including these people in:

- Sunday lunch
- popping round for a drink
- sending the children off to visit them
- school assemblies if there's a gap and a space beside you
- weekends away
- your birthday-card and postcard lists.

Becoming Part of Your Local Community

Feeling like a part of your local community helps you and your family put down roots and gives you a great sense of belonging and looking out for each other – not to mention the perks of advice on pruning, chats about council services and the weather, borrowing emergency corkscrews and watching babies grow up almost before your eyes. You can feel lonely and isolated as a single mum, but a chat with a neighbour, however brief and casual, can make you feel like you really are home and belong in your neighbourhood. We're not suggesting you embark on a door-to-door campaign of forcing cups of tea on unsuspecting neighbours, but more of adopting a mindset that means you smile at neighbours, the shop assistant you always get your paper and diet soda from, the man at the flower stall, the woman at the ticket office and so on. The 'Morning, how are you?', 'Lovely weather!', 'Bet you're pleased the day's nearly over' type of conversations you and your children have with people will help you to become a part of the fabric and you'll soon stop feeling like you're different or being judged or sticking out like a sore thumb.

Here are our ideas of things you could do:

- Get in your garden – prune, water, tinker about and say more than 'Hello' to a neighbour (this is easiest if you're tending your front garden!).
- Clean your windows or the front door – anything that means you've got time to exchange pleasantries with someone who passes by.
- Sit in the sun on your doorstep or, if you're like Kate, get a chair and sit outside your home while the children play on the pavement. All children love to play on the pavement.
- Invite the neighbour from two doors down who always says hello, has children of similar ages and seems really nice to come round for a cup of coffee.
- Find your local playgroup and go four times on the trot.
- Get in with the PTA (even if it's just to man a stall at the school fête).
- Get an allotment, take the children with you and dig and plant at the weekend.
- Join your children up at a local tennis, rugby, football club – you get the picture, any sport where there's the opportunity to skulk on the sidelines supporting them and chatting to other parents. *NB:* tennis clubs are notoriously social, and there are always the tennis coaches to think about!

Becoming Part of a Bigger Family

It's a wonderful thing when a small family can be likened to a branch of an old oak tree. Solid and sturdy, the family tree can help to give your gang a place within a bigger family and help them to learn about their roots. A good part of this is about getting to know the cast of recent years, so why not start with a bit of genealogy? It's all the rage at the moment. Writing a family tree for both sides of the children's family can be fun and interesting. They just love seeing the same names crop up, and want to know more about family dramas, such as ladies dying in childbirth and so on, as well as finding out where people lived and what they did. Names, dates and figures, which may seem on the dry side, really spice up the history of the family – and it's great for the children to be able to see themselves as part of this 'tree'.

Putting colour into the picture is where the current members of both sides of the family come in, and it comes from all the little pieces of information that make you feel safe and secure in the knowledge that you come from a long line of people who hate cheese, love eating raw potatoes and onions and are tone-deaf – all very reassuring when these traits pop up in your own family!

For some of you it's probably too painful to talk about your and their dad's story, or about his childhood, particularly if you're feeling badly treated by him. For the rest of us it's probably more a matter of forcing yourself, as it's not going to be a favourite topic, but the more you can bring yourself to divulge family tit-bits like 'Dad's great uncle Caractacus was a keen sailor, too,' the better. Of course there will be much that you don't know about or may just never get round to saying. This is where the extended family can help enormously.

Pack the children off with an uncle on their dad's side and get him chatting about when he and Dad were young and the antics they got up to (or if they weren't the sort of boys who got up to antics, then perhaps the stamp collection they had, or the trains they spotted?).

Get Granny and Granddad to get the photos out of when Dad was a baby, growing up, wearing velvet jackets and growing a beard, and get everyone talking about the 'old days' – the children will be engaged and ask questions and generally lap up their history.

Don't forget it's not all about finding out about their dad's child-hood and family history. They need to know yours, too, and as your husband isn't there to prompt you to reminisce, or to encourage you to tell them about your most embarrassing moment, it's a very good idea to get your brothers, sisters and parents to tell your stories, to show your old school books, holiday snaps, etc. The children need to see you in context, too, and to learn how you handled things, what mistakes you made, how you survived and became who you are today. Don't forget that you'll be their most influential role model, so showing them how *not* to do it as is important as showing them how!

> All that rubbish has passed. That's what happens in divorce,
> it's just emotions you go through. We started out as friends
> and we have wonderful children. At the end of the day it's
> all about families. Jude and I will always be family.
> Sadie Frost, *Grazia* 10th December 2007

> You teach children by example. I don't employ a nanny.
> We eat together. We discuss everything. I never hit them.
> My ultimate punishment is: no friends at the weekend.
> They've turned out to be wonderful people.
> Jerry Hall, © *Guardian News and Media Ltd,* 2007

> *[Dame Judi Dench feels part of her grandparenting role is to
> educate. She says:]* Sam calls me 'Ma'. I'm like an old chief
> in his life. I think being a grandma is great fun and I took
> Sam to Stratford with me when I was with the Royal
> Shakespeare Company. I wanted him to have a chance to
> understand a bit about his past.
> Dame Judi Dench, *Chronicle Live* December 2007

Chapter 7

DADS

Dad Is Important

This is the section of the book where we really put our cards on the table and emphasize the importance to the children of a healthy, loving, positive and ongoing relationship with their father. If Dad is struggling, then we will show you how to help him. If you're making things difficult for Dad, then we will offer some tough talk which WILL be worth it in the end, so, please, all of you hang on in there!

Maybe you've been let down massively, maybe you really think very little of the geezer. NONE of this matters a jot. Dad is Dad and nothing is going to change that, and he's important to the children (and if he's not, he should be).

We've an incredibly simple and indisputable view of parents: children are created 50% from Mum and 50% from Dad, and this is one of the ways they see themselves. So to have a negative relationship or view of either of their parents will put a strain on the children. Be aware that children who are not able to develop a strong relationship with their father may feel abandoned, unloved, unlovable and rejected. You don't have to be Sigmund Freud to realize that any dent in the way youngsters perceive themselves is not a good thing and may have repercussions throughout their lives. That's it, really; that's why we think it's a good idea to have Dad around.

No, not everyone gets on with their parents, even in two-parent families, and you can't make it happen, but as a mother you should do everything in your power to support and help the children's relationship with Dad.

Separated dads have the most amazing ability to be fabulous fathers; they have the ability to be better dads than they were as part of a couple. By spending time on their own with the children, trying harder than they did before, and without the buffer of another adult around, oftentimes men are forced to work out a new relationship that can be massively rewarding for them. Even though they may feel like part-time parents, they can still have a real and special bond with their children.

Dear Kate and Emily,
My husband and I separated four years ago. We had grown apart and he had little interest in our three boys. However, our split has turned him into a far better dad than he was before. He spends time with them and they now have bonded into a gang of four, camping, watching the football and having fun. I know this sounds bad, but it makes me feel very irritated and, I would even go as far as to say, deeply pissed off! Why the hell couldn't he have made this sort of an effort when we were together?
Love,
He Was Useless of Haselmere

Dear He Was Useless,

He's doing it because he has to. Who else cooks, cleans and entertains them on his weekends? We suspect that you know you need to get a grip. Yes, it's sad that it took your separation to allow this to happen, but to be honest, being a good dad and a good husband don't go hand in hand. We can understand why you may feel a bit put out, but do keep this to yourself. You don't want to spoil the great time that the boys have when they spend time with their father. Rejoice in the success that the two of you are making of co-parenting. Being a parent is not a competitive sport. No further questions, Your Honour!

Love, Kate and Emily

What Dad Brings to the Party

- Fathers provide an equal dose of identity, history, character, belonging, physical and personal connection that makes all of us feel whole and grounded.
- Fathers provide a second layer of protection and support, love and discipline.
- Fathers have a different take on parenting. They think further into the future about bringing up their children, focusing more on the long-term development and teaching the children to become more independent.
- Fathers encourage their children to take more risks, which is vital in the growing-up process. We know it's true, but even as we pen this we're dreading an upcoming father-and-son potholing weekend!
- Men and women have a different take on the world. Having a father involved encourages a more balanced view of the world and greater understanding of men. This is important for children as they grow up and develop relationships.

If all this is sticking in your throat, spend some time thinking about it a little more and try to understand your reaction. Here are some questions to get you thinking:

1. Write down the disadvantages to YOU of encouraging your ex to be an involved parent. Would your children agree with you? Why? Why not?
2. Write down at least one advantage to:
   • your CHILDREN of encouraging your ex to be an involved parent
   • YOU of encouraging your ex to be an involved parent.
3. Check that what you're writing is based on your ex as a parent, not on them as someone who hurt you, or whom you hurt, or who is a prize plonker.

As a general rule of thumb, know for a fact that:

• Children have one mum and one dad; both are part of who they are.
• Mum and Dad are irreplaceable and can't be divorced.
• Children don't like it when their parents are criticized.
• Children don't like to feel they have to take sides.
• Children benefit from the love of two parents.
• Children want permission to be able to love both parents.
• Children will grow up and work it all out in the end, so sabotage the relationship at your peril.

Statistics show that four out of seven dads lose touch with their children within a couple of years of a break-up. Your children don't want their dad to be one of these four. Before you can prevent it happening, you need to think why it might ever happen and what you can do to make sure it doesn't come to this.

Why on Earth Might a Dad Give Up?

- If he's not encouraged and made to feel uncomfortable.
- If he's treated aggressively or forced to confront difficult feelings.
- If the children are reluctant to be with him. Be honest, we all know that children are hard work when they behave in this way. This makes life difficult and the stress of the situation can lead to him giving up. He may believe he's doing the right thing for everyone by reducing stress and making everyone happier.
- As part of a mum-and-dad set up he may have taken a bit of a backseat on the domestic front. He may not have bothered to learn what to do, how to talk to the children or how to play with them.
- As a single mother does so much of the parenting, they get better at it and can view fathers as less competent. When this happens, a pattern is set in which the mother does more, learns more, feels more confident, and continues to take on more and more responsibility for the children. The father in that situation does less, learns less, and feels less capable of providing daily care. The mother parents him out of the picture.
- Constant nagging and badgering for money have proven to be an effective way of sending a man to ground.
- The guilt or heartbreak that may be associated with returning to the scene of failure may lead to a misguided belief on Dad's part that all will be better if the slate is wiped clean and he stays away permanently. There's a view that men who cut and run adjust better psychologically to a split than those who hang around getting involved. We find it hard to believe that intelligent parents are really and truly able, if they stop and think, to feel good about abandoning their children.

Then there's the part mothers can play in sidelining and alienating fathers. First off, have a look at any elements of your behaviour that may be undermining him and making his job harder. Maybe you're subtly involved in subterfuge? Have a very serious talk with yourself:

are you pushing Dad off the scene? Read this list and if bells of recognition ring, then a bit of soul-searching might be needed!

- You want to start a new life and think it'll be easier without him.
- You feel so disappointed in him that you feel he's unworthy to be Dad and doesn't deserve the children.
- What's the big deal? He shouldn't have left in the first place. He made his bed, he can lie in it.
- You're finding it difficult to cope, and contact with your children's father is difficult and upsetting for you. He's a reminder of failure and maybe rejection or guilt.
- You're jealous of the gifts he gives your children as you can't afford them; in fact, the children end up demanding more from you and you feel that you can't compete.
- You want him to realize what he has done and that he has to pay a price. He can't have his cake and eat it.
- He's rubbish and you're over-critical of his attempts, it's easier to do everything yourself. Dad has a different lifestyle and is a plonker and the children are better off with you and Mr New Squeeze.

Be honest. Is it easier, less painful or unpleasant if you keep Dad out of the picture? Is it your way of coping with the situation? This is the worst bit about being a single parent – you break up with someone, you hate them, love them, want to obliterate them from your life – but you CAN'T because you've had children together, so you're still tied to each other for life. It can be some people's worst nightmare.

Even if you're OK about your break-up, it can seem easier to sort of forget about the children's dad. You know what they say – 'Out of sight, out of mind.' We can all get so busy in the day-to-day of running our own lives that it doesn't even cross our minds to get the children to phone their dad, drop him an email, etc. And imagine how much harder this is to do if their dad lives on the other side of the world? Do you think to keep him in touch with news about the children, where you've moved to, etc.?

He may be a pretty apathetic father, but are you being equally apathetic about keeping in touch? Because until your children reach adulthood and become independent and responsible for their own lives, you're responsible for doing all you can to keep their dad in their lives.

How to Help Dad Become Involved

- Learn to communicate effectively and positively with Dad, using the principles of the co-parenting chapter. Think about a code of conduct and, however bad things may have got, start again to try and find a way of working together.
- Make it easy for him to stay involved. If he's not being proactive, guide him and suggest things to do and trips that you know will be a success. If he hasn't had much experience being with them on his own, help him (leave lists, tips, etc. if he wants them).
- Give him lots of notice of school events.
- Get the children to communicate with him: if they want to talk to him, let them phone; if they have a piece of good news at school, why not say 'Give Dad a ring and let him know'?
- Make sure that the children have a positive view of Dad. NEVER trash him in their hearing.
- Make sure the children know that you're happy that they're going to be with Dad, having a good time. They may not want to go if they think you're worried or will miss them.
- Keep Dad up to speed on your children's lives: when they're having problems, when they're taking exams as well as other bits and bobs that are important to them.
- Remember that the differences, as well as the similarities, between parents are good for children. Remember that there are many right ways to raise children and that your child benefits from more than just your way. Allow for loving differences in the ways your ex-partner parents.
- Each parent deserves a chance to develop his or her relationship

with the children. Most of us do better at learning the art of parenting when we don't have someone looking over our shoulders as we go.

Things within Your Control and Things beyond It

There's something called 'circles of influence' which divide our world into things we can influence and things we can't. It helps us focus on the things we can do something about and stop wasting energy and time on the things we haven't got a cat in hell's chance of doing anything about. Thinking like this was a revelation to us as, all of a sudden, the things that had been gnawing away at us – the worry about whether their dad would relocate to the Outer Hebrides, go AWOL, lose the children on a trip, not cook the chicken properly, etc. – were lifted because we realized we couldn't influence them. What a weight was lifted! So reduce your worries by establishing what you can influence and what you can't.

How Well Do I Expect Their Dad to Behave?

No unrealistic demands or overly high expectations here! Make a list of your expectations, and then re-read each one, matching it with how you'll behave and, if you can't match the expectation, moderate it. Here are some examples; you'll soon get the idea.

Keeping your expectations sensible
Our top tip to stop you judging their dad too harshly and for keeping your expectations under control is this:

- Pretend you're judging your own parents' behaviour towards you. For example, if your children's dad hasn't phoned for three days and you find yourself saying 'He's forgotten them and doesn't care any more,' think what your reaction would be if it was your mum or dad who had behaved like this. You'd probably pick up the phone yourself and call them – so why not ring him for the children? Or you'd remember that they were busy, or you'd told them that you were out and about for most of the week.

MY EXPECTATIONS OF THEIR DAD	I'LL DO THIS (so this is really how I can expect him to behave)
To be punctual	I'll be as punctual as I can, but I'll always tell him if I'm held up and leave a key with a neighbour so he'll always be able to get in.
To stick to what we've agreed about weekends	I'll stick to our agreed arrangements, but if something comes up like a family reunion I'll let him know as soon as I do and ask to swap weekends. I won't give him less than a month's notice.
To spend all his holiday time with the children	I know the children love holidays and seeing him, so I'll let him have them whenever he can in the holidays. I accept that he might not want to spend all of his holiday time with them, though.
Not to flaunt new girl-friends in front of me	I'll tell him if my boyfriend is going to be around when he is. I won't force them on each other, or show off or rub it in when I see him.

When Dad Is Around But Not Accessible

From the people we've met it doesn't seem that uncommon for fathers and mothers to end up living at opposite ends of the country, or even in different countries. As the world shrinks, more long-distance relationships are formed. It means that there'll be an increasing number of single mums bringing up their children with largely absent dads. It makes co-parenting all the more challenging and means that you need to be more superhuman than the rest of us, because not only will you have the children full-on, practically all the time, you'll also have to deal with your children's upset when they see their dad and have to say goodbye to him again. Seeing your child upset like this can break your heart and make you question whether it really isn't better for the children not to see their dad. A child psychologist told us that, though it's painful for the child as they're effectively mourning the loss of their dad afresh each time he goes, it's still *more* damaging for them not to see him at all.

As the one left holding the proverbial baby, you need to realize it's their mourning which is making them have tantrums, swear at you, kick you, hate you and so on. It's going to be wearing, but just grit your teeth and be loving, kind and constant. Don't over-compensate, just be reassuringly normal and they'll settle down. One mum we know takes a week off work when her daughter comes back from seeing her dad in America to help settle her back down again.

For one teenage boy, having a dad who lives in Newquay is now a bit of a plus as he spends every summer holiday there, and has a fantastic time. Because he spends a couple of months with his dad every year he feels he knows him well, and they have a very good, close relationship.

Ideally, try to encourage lots of little, easy and regular contact. Here are some ways of keeping Dad on the radar screen when he lives far away, as well as ideas to keep in regular and constant touch:

- letters and postcards
- get Dad to make story tapes for bedtime
- have photos up in the children's rooms
- phone calls
- web cams
- email
- Skype (phoning via the Internet, apparently. We're too techno-phobic to know how it works, other than if you and the person you're calling get the Internet and some software, you can use Skype to talk at Internet prices – i.e. free!)
- MSN
- A granny we read about kept in touch with her grandchildren in

America through the children's network site, Penguinland. Everyone is a penguin, with their own name, colour, etc., so she'd meet her grandchildren for a chat on an iceberg!

* Facebook and all the other friends' networks might work for older children. It can't be a bad thing to 'talk' to your children through the channel that they use to talk to their friends. Our gut feeling is that you'll get more out of your children and know them better if you do it on their terms and join their world rather than expect them to come to yours.

So help and suggest to Dad that you would like to use some of these ideas to get regular communication channels open.

Turning to you and your life, you may feel in a bit of a different group and not a 'regular fry' single parent. To all intents and purposes you're bringing up your child alone, you don't get weekends off, you get the brunt of all the aggro and maybe you feel that Dad hasn't enough day-to-day knowledge of the children to be of much use. In this regard you may feel more of a widow than a single parent. Do crack on with the 'When Dad's Not Around' section (see page 147-148), which has some ideas that might help, and also remember that your children do have a dad and the more he can mean to them, wherever he is, the better.

Dear Kate and Emily,

My ex moved to the US a year ago and has been back to see our daughter once for four days in that time. He's now proposing that she fly to San Francisco to spend Christmas and New Year with him.

I've since found out that he has moved in with his new family – separated woman and her daughter – and wishes to show our daughter his new life. While I believe that it's great and fantastic that he wishes to spend some time with our daughter, I've some concerns. At three, how will she cope with the long flight and then being put into situations with people she doesn't know? If she does go, how can I best prepare her? How can I make the whole experience a better one for her and her relationship with her daddy?

I've already tried talking to my ex about this and all I'm getting back from him is 'You're just trying to ruin my relationship with my daughter'!

Love,
Long Haul from Leicester

Dear Long Haul,

Loads of what you've written sounds so positive and great, you clearly have a genuine understanding of the importance of your child's relationship with her father and you sound totally supportive, which is fab.

Now to the nuts and bolts. How about going as well? Your daughter is really very young and you must both stand back and look at this from her perspective. If this geographic arrangement is for the foreseeable future, then it'll be great for your child to be able to enjoy a good relationship with her dad and her American family throughout her whole childhood, adolescence and adult life. Think about this (both of you as parents) and work together to ease her into the whole thing in a gentle age-appropriate fashion, letting the situation evolve in a happy, positive way. Remember for all three of you it could be great if this works and a US trip develops into a great annual experience. In short, you both want her to go willingly, happily and full of excitement in the future, so tread gently at the start. So how about flying with her and staying nearby if possible for at least a while? Take a pile of books and DVDs (sorry, it's not going to be your best Christmas, unless you can get a mate to come with you!).

As far as preparing her, get her dad to take lots of photos of his home, inside and out, or even send a video film of the house right down to where she will be sleeping. Hopefully her dad is able to do this; he may feel a bit of an idiot at the outset, he may not want you to see it, but that is not the point, the point is to prepare the ground for the stay and to make his home seem more familiar to his daughter. Also, give him full and detailed descriptions of food that she will (and won't) eat as well as details of fave films, books, characters, etc. so that some of these could be there to greet her when she arrives. Maybe he could chat and play with her via a webcam?

Love, Kate and Emily

Staying at Dad's

For the vast majority of children and dads, the times they spend together are fun, exciting, precious and happy. It isn't often that problems arise around staying at his, but when they do it's usually for one of these reasons:

- The children want to stay behind because there's a party they want to go to.
- They feel ill and want to be 'mothered'.
- They think their loyalties lie with their mum and she'll miss them.
- There's been a change in either home and it has unsettled them (new partners, babies, new house, etc.).

Here are some ways to help make going to see Dad go smoothly:

- Organize a schedule way in advance and put it up for all to see.
- Talk about your child's life with their dad (nicely!).
- Spend some time at handover with Dad to ease transition.

- Don't make it possible for the child to undermine or manipulate you about seeing their dad.
- Stand firm on the importance of seeing Dad.
- When the child returns home, be interested in what they've done, let them tell you about it just as if they had spent time with, say, your parents or a friend.
- Be pleased for them if they have had a great time and let them know that you've had a good time without them.
- Talk up going to stay with their dad like mad.

When children do put their feet down and refuse to go and see their dad, it's not usually about him, it's about the fact that friends have become more important than family. As has having their things around them. Why on earth would they want to be parted from the PlayStation and their friends? It's a no-brainer to a teenager. To their dad, desperate to see them, it's a no-brainer too, as they scream inside with the pain of rejection 'because you're my child!'

So if a sulking child is not happy about going, clutching onto bathroom taps in desperation, refusing to budge, try and encourage their father to realize that this is not about him, it's about missing their day-to-day life. Then, why not suggest:

- He makes friends with people who have similar-aged children around.
- He gets them to feel part of where he lives by signing them up for Saturday football, swimming lessons, etc. – anything that's regular, normal and involves local children.
- He shares a hobby with them or encourages them to develop one that they do with him, not with their mum.
- He makes his home a real home for them by doing all the normal things with them like homework, getting their hair cut, buying school shoes and letting them put their posters up in their bedroom so that it feels like theirs.
- He tries to keep up with a modern-day child's needs and fads. Get Sky if it's a 'must have' in every young person's house!

- He tries to make it so that coming to his house feels like they're going to their other home, then, as they get older, they'll still come off their own bat because they have friends and a life there, too.

And finally on the subject of seeing their dad: 'visits' is the wrong word to use for describing your children's weekends or other time at Dad's. 'Visits' sends messages we hadn't even thought about. It seems obvious now we've had it pointed out: as soon as you call them visits, the children become 'visitors' in their other parent's home. Children can cope with the idea of two homes, so use that. So instead of 'visit', they can 'spend time with' Dad, or 'go to Dad's', or 'have a Dad weekend'. And now we think about it, we wonder if 'visits' helps to reinforce in our own heads the feeling that we're the main parent, we're where it happens, and encourages us to think of the one being 'visited' as an unequal partner in this parenting lark?

Dear Kate and Emily,

I am seven years post-separation and five years post-divorce and it was all very difficult at the time. I've four girls, now 16, 13, 12 and 10. The oldest is the only one who sees her dad regularly, although even that now seems to be breaking down. He lives locally but hasn't seen three of my girls for almost three years. He refuses to see the girls without his new wife being present, and they won't see him with her because they feel she's too controlling. I struggled initially and encouraged all the girls to go, but after two years of tears, anxiety, etc. gave up as they reached an age where the cajoling and the promises of having a good time didn't wash! I feel very sad for them as they're missing out on a fulfilling relationship both with him and their grand-parents. I am also sad for him as the girls are such wonderful people and growing up and away so fast. As time goes by I feel that it'll become more difficult for them to rekindle their

relationship. I am not able to approach him to resolve problems, and although I've tried to write to him he accuses me of interfering. Historically he has been unwilling to communicate with me in any way and if I do see him he ignores me even when I've got the girls with me. I would love the girls to see their dad. Any ideas or is it too late?
Love,
Kids Off Dad of Kidderminster

Dear Kids Off Dad,
You're right, both the dad and the girls are missing out, and so are you with no support in bringing them up, weekends off, etc. But co-parenting is more than the girls going round to see their dad — it's about him being involved in their school life, interests, life decisions, etc. We know that it's easy to forget (or to just stop) including the dad in things like Christmas concerts, parents' evenings, school fairs, sports days, sending copies of the latest school photo, etc. You probably stopped doing this long ago, but how about starting to invite him? It might be an easier way back in for him and the girls. Email him or text him with the idea. Make no big thing about it; if he doesn't reply, text or email again and let him know that if you don't hear you'll assume he can't make it this time but that you'll contact him in future about any events as they come up — don't give up.
Then there are the grandparents. Again, contact the dad and tell him you've been thinking what a long time it's been since the girls saw them, and that you wondered if he had any plans to get them all together. If not, then say you thought you'd get in touch with them and perhaps see if they were free one Sunday for the girls to pop round to see them. It may also be that getting to know their grandparents and more about their dad will help them to warm towards him again. You see, we don't really believe that children stop loving their parents — we think they might get hurt

by them so turn away from them to hide their hurt, or they may feel torn and feel they have to take sides, and that going to see their dad would be disloyal to you. Please think about that, because you can stop them feeling like that and tell them it's all right and that you're happy for them to go. Our guess is that small children who refuse to see their dad are doing it not because they hate him, have a horrid time, etc., but because they're picking up a vibe that says 'If I go to Dad, then Mum will be sad and hurt.' Could this could be a hangover from the horrible divorce time?

Love, Kate and Emily

Ideas for Making Handover Time Easier

Handover is always tricky with emotional and tired children (and parents!). It can be a flashpoint for many, especially for those parents who are still effectively at war. Here are some tips from others on how they try to minimize the stress and ease the process:

- I don't tell the children when he's due, exactly. I'll say 'the morning' rather than '9.30' so that if he's late they're not disappointed.
- When he's late I have to remind myself that it's really not major, and if I've managed the children's expectations properly they won't be upset so why should I be?
- I make a point of asking my ex some innocuous question, just polite chit-chat, really, to lighten the atmosphere and make it easier for the children.
- I make sure there's another adult in the house at pick-up and drop-off times as it makes my ex behave better.

Some people have rituals that help the children settle down quickly when they come back after time at Dad's:

- We have a hug on the sofa.
- I run a big bubble bath and we all get in.
- We play a card game before bedtime.
- I really hug them and stroke their hair a lot.
- We put on our favourite CD and dance like loonies.

It's so obvious, but don't forget that children, too, can feel rejected and protect themselves from being hurt any more by pretending they don't care and shutting down. They may refuse to go at handover time. We've heard some very heartbreaking stories of children having to be physically dragged out of the house to go to their dad.

You need to nip this in the bud, because dragging a screaming child who's refusing to go to her dad's feels to many mothers like child cruelty, so they just can't do it. To the father who's come to pick up his child, it can be seen as a sign that the mother has turned his child away from him, that the child hates him, that it's not worth seeing the child for a while. There's a risk that this 'for a while' will turn into a very long time unless you both try to sort it out.

Children pick up on vibes. If 'Daddy broke Mummy's heart' and Mummy's always crying, then they won't want to leave you. They'll want to protect you and know that you're OK, rather than worry about you when they're at Dad's. Going off with their father can make them feel like a traitor, so it's up to you to make sure they know you're OK.

Dear Kate and Emily,
I don't know what to do. When my husband has the children he insists I drive over an hour to meet him at a services near him to hand over the children. The real problem is that he tells me what time I have to be there with very little notice, and threatens me that if I'm late he'll drive off because he's not waiting and thinks I've got nothing else to do, so can manage it. He says that he pays me to look after the children, so doesn't see why

this isn't part of my 'job'. I sort of see what he means, but the times can be inconvenient and traffic's unpredictable, so I worry so much about being late. The children are taken from one car to another like possessions, it's horrible and I don't know what to do.
Love,
Handover Hell of Hampton Wick

Dear Handover Hell,
Other than appealing to his better nature by putting forward very practical reasons for any change in the plan that would benefit him as well as you, there's little you can do as the priority has to be the children seeing their dad and you can't play games with that. But there might be alternatives that would work better, like a nicer handover spot with a play area so you could get there a little early when you take the children and they could play while keeping an eye out for Dad. Or let them play there before you take them home to make the transition pleasanter?
Love, Kate and Emily

When Dad's Not Around

In some situations there's no Dad around and Mum is bringing up the children without Dad completely. These single mums don't get weekends off, another parent to share the tasks and responsibility with, and get no financial help at all. Neither of us is in this situation but we've met several people who are. They're among the most feisty, courageous and protective mothers we know, and are often coping so well. However, as Dad may be a distant memory, becoming dimmer for Mum, in all probability he will become increasingly important to the children as they start to think and wonder, imagine and dream.

Whatever happened, you should reassure them that this is not their fault. This is a big one, and may well require some extra help at some point. In the meantime keep positive, keep all the reasons for the situation a million miles away from the children.

There's a natural, deep-rooted urge in all of us to know where we come from. This means that children, even grown-up children, will want to know as much about both parents as they can. It doesn't matter if they have never seen their father, or don't even know his name – they will always want to know where they came from and who created them. We want to urge you to gather as much information, as trivial or irrelevant as it may seem, so that if the children really want to know about him in the future you can produce something, even if it's just a file of bits and bobs. For your part, knowing that you've some answers will be greatly reassuring and make your children's job, should they wish or need to find him in the future, so much easier.

Children Will Always Want to Know Their Father

When it's just been you and the children for as long as you can all remember, you tend to look at your children and think how happy you all are together. You can't help but think that as their dad is barely even a memory and that they've never known any different, they'll not need to know about their dad. Surely if they were interested they'd ask? You're very close after all, aren't you? They can talk to you about anything, can't they? Not necessarily. We read so often about adults who search for their birth parents, delve into their family history and only feel complete and at peace within themselves when they have satiated their animal-like hunger for knowing where they came from. So remember:

- Your children will always want to know about their dad.
- Talk about him in a way that lets them know it's OK to want to know about him.

- You'll have to start the conversations.
- Actively encourage their questions. Even if you don't know the answers, at least you know what's on their mind and can help them to deal with it.

Co-parenting Alone ... Yes, It Is Possible

In Chapter 5 (Co-parenting) we talked about the importance of having your own code of conduct to follow when you're dealing with the children's father, as it'll help you to consciously keep your behaviour in check. Now, co-parenting with an absent dad is a whole different kettle of fish, and some would say a daft idea given there's no co-parent! However, that's not strictly true – there is a co-parent, he's just not taking part. But the code of conduct still stands. It's vital that you set yourself some guidelines on how you'll behave about your children's father.

He might not be around, but you still need to respect the fact that he's your children's dad and he'll be a hero to them. This is a code of conduct we wrote for a couple who are co-parenting, but you can read it and see how easily it applies to a situation where Dad is absent, too:

- Don't criticize or be disparaging about him.
- Handle all the upset and history away from the children. They'll pick up on vibes.
- Talk positively about him and your relationship regardless of how brief it was.
- Keep him alive for the children.
- Understand him and give him credit wherever you can, even mentioning physical traits ('You've a twinkle in your eye just like your dad.').
- Don't take advantage of his absence to promote your own cause.
- Help him to be the best parent he can be even in his absence: pass on any of his good values, use his life story to show his children how to handle life, etc.

When the father is never seen, your children will rely on you and other relatives to tell them about him. If children with no contact with their father hear only that he's bad, they'll end up believing that they come from someone who couldn't, and wouldn't, stay at home to care for them, so surely didn't love them, then. Imagine how painful a conclusion this is for a child to come to.

If you say good things about the absent father, for example that when you were together there were some good times, and that he loved his baby and/or you (if he never saw the baby), then your child has a chance of having a picture of a good father in mind.

This means, of course, that you need to be brave and actively force yourself to behave in a way that goes against your own emotions. Keep in mind that while it may be incredibly painful to remember your child's dad, this will also give you the ability to make sense of your broken relationship with him. It means that a bad father can still be understood and not just rejected out of hand, or that a good one can be remembered. Your job is to allow your children to know their father, not to reject him on their behalf.

Dear Kate and Emily,
As soon as I became pregnant my then boyfriend made his excuses and wasn't seen for dust. He hasn't met, or shown any interest in, his son who's now six. I am very angry and bitter about the way my son's father has behaved, but I know I shouldn't let that affect what my son thinks of him, so I tuck him up each night, give him a kiss and tell him that 'Daddy kisses him too and loves him very much.' Am I doing enough?
Love,
Telling White Lies of Whitstable

Dear Telling White Lies,
First we must congratulate you on doing the best you can for your son by keeping your views about your ex-boyfriend to yourself! That really deserves a gold star. You just need to think through exactly what it is you're telling your son, i.e. that a dad shows his love by making no contact with him. Is that really what you want him to think love is? If you can talk about his dad to him without any bitterness, then tell him 'Dad stories' — nice things you remember about him — and try to explain to him why he isn't around. You know your son best, but something along the lines of 'Some people get scared about being a parent and don't think they'll do a good job, so they think their child will be happier being brought up without them, though you can be sure he thinks about you a lot, he just trusts me to bring you up to be a fine young man — and we'll show him how right he is, shall we?' Best of luck, Kate and Emily

What can I tell them? – I don't know anything about him

You probably know more than you think. For example, you know how you met, things you did together, places you went. Even if your relationship was short, you'll have something to say, so write it down as if you've been asked to write an essay about it. Imagine you've got to write 20 pages on the subject and can put anything in, however vague. 'We met in a bar and he had a pint of lager with pork scratchings; we talked about x, y and z.' Why not do it now before you forget? And then, once you have explored the depths of your brain for everything you know and every part of 'your' story, you can take up the 'extremely tenuous' route – like the history of the Macdonald clan because his surname was Macdonald! Really, anything, just fill the pages and your children will have something at least that starts to fill in the gaps about their father and heritage.

You'll find that not only is it lovely to remember the early happy days, but it can be very therapeutic too. Even silly things like what you both had to drink, what you danced to, what he wore, what you thought when you first saw him – these are all things that will help your children bring their dad to life, and they're all memories that no one else can give your child. If your children never do find their dad, then these memories are going to be all they will have.

Have you got a picture of him? Has anyone else? Mention him when something triggers your memory; ask your child if he'd like to hear 'the Daddy story' again. Of course it'll depend on your history, but there must be something that is factual, and paints at least a bit of a picture (it doesn't have to be a perfect one!) that your children can hear as they grow up. The story can help to explain why he isn't around now, as managing children's sense of rejection must be the hardest bit.

Practical Tips
- Try and find contact details for him, and check them once a year.
- If you can't contact the father, can you find any of his family? His parents or siblings?
- Use friends you knew at the time to help you: someone might know someone or something.
- If the father is from another country and you've lost the trail, you could still introduce the country and culture to your child.
- Google him.
- Do you know the industry he worked in? The school or college he went to? Have you got any contacts there, or can you look on Facebook, Friends Reunited, etc.?

Remember, there's stalking in order to name and shame and then there's simply trying to find someone! Tread carefully, as his friends and family will feel protective of his privacy and not want to be disloyal to him. So explain that this is only about being able to give his child some background about him and contact details so they can find him when they're old enough.

Meeting Dad for the First Time

You've found their dad, or their dad has found you, and he wants to see his child. You make arrangements, you tell your child and help to prepare them for the meeting, and allow them to be excited, nervous, apprehensive, etc.

Just a word of warning: sometimes these meetings don't happen because the father cancels. Perhaps he gets cold feet, or perhaps he feels it will open a can of worms and complicate things; who knows? But it can happen. Sometimes the visits are a massive disappointment to the child, probably because Dad isn't who they had imagined him to be, and it's not the beautiful reunion they had been imagining all this time. Hero Dad turns out to be dullish and boring with a comb-over and dodgy walk. Now, you probably knew he'd be like that (or had an inkling) – so you should prepare your child for the reality, as they're bound to be imagining a demi-god as their dad!

We don't know the answers; only you know your child and situation, so you must take your own counsel. It's just that one little boy we met still doesn't understand why his father didn't turn up to meet him when he said he would. What do you say? How can you explain it? How can you protect a child from that hurt and pain? Do you tell them about the visit beforehand, or do you wait until you're really sure it'll happen? Managing expectations about when they're going to meet their dad for one time only is a little different from preparing them for a dad who is coming over for bathtime tomorrow. All we can really say is think about it.

And remember, this little boy we've mentioned still wants to know why his dad didn't show, and is still trying to work it out in his head six years on. The need doesn't go away, and even though you too might not know why he never came back, you need to talk to your child about it to let them wander around the subject, and help them come to terms with it.

Good Male Role Models Are Important

Most single mums have worried at one time or another that their children don't have a male role model in their lives now that their dad has gone. This is compounded by the fact that their dad may not have been an ideal role model in the first place.

First, take heart: role models are important and will be found in every aspect of your children's life. Girls and boys both need men and to learn what it is to be a man, but this lesson can be easily taught without a father living at home.

You can help them to learn what good male qualities are by pointing out the positive qualities in men you see on a day-to-day basis. This means that even if you're buying your son football boots and the salesman is especially attentive or friendly, point this trait out by mentioning what a helpful person he is.

As your children grow up, investigate local activities or sports clubs that they could join that are run or taught by a man (for example, Emily's children did karate and football, which they both enjoyed and Emily liked as it brought them into contact with good male role models that they respected and listened to). These male-led activities might be a particularly good idea if the children have exclusively women teachers at school (and most of them will). Remember to try not to show a negative attitude towards men, even if you became a single mother out of the most excruciating circumstances.

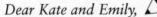

Dear Kate and Emily,
The children's dad isn't around and hasn't been since my eldest was three. I don't worry about her so much now as she's a lovely 11-year-old and we enjoy shopping and watching the same sort of TV programmes and films. My son's nine, though, and really misses having a man around to talk and play with. I worry about him but don't think there's anything I can do. What do you think?
Love,
No Dad of Nuneaton

Dear No Dad,

You're doing well with your daughter, not because she's necessarily easier or better company than your son, but because you understand her and share her girlie interests. It won't come so naturally to you, but you need to arrange some quality 'boy' time with your son, just as you've got quality 'girl' time with your daughter. How about watching a sport together, a boy-type museum trip, a visit to his football team's grounds, swimming, a kick around in the park? Ask your son what he'd like to do with you one afternoon and do it. You'll be in Dad role, indulging his male interests and showing an interest in him just as a dad would. Then think about the activity that your son enjoys most. Is this something that you're good at, or is there an adult male friend, godfather or relative who could do it with him?

Love, Kate and Emily

Helping Your Son Become a Well-balanced Man

As well as letting your child seek his own heroes and role models, there are things you can do to allow him to be male. Whether or not you've a man around to show him the ropes, your son can grow up to be an emotionally healthy male just as many boys of single mums have already done. Some useful tips about ways to treat our sons are:

- Accept your son's differences.
- Be a little creative in helping your child learn male things. For instance, many single mothers report concern over their sons using the potty while sitting, or playing with their make-up. Chances are your child won't spend the rest of his life peeing sitting down while wearing mascara. But if you want to get a head start on defining the differences between male and female characteristics, try this. Set out a little basket just for him. Fill it

with a mock razor, gentle shaving cream, watered-down cologne, his toothbrush, toothpaste and a comb. Let him know this is what most men do every morning to their faces.

- Teach him your values, but let him express them uniquely. He's a male and will respond to emotional situations somewhat differently than you might.

- If your boy is really active, get some exercise equipment for his room for rainy days. Exercise is critical for all children, but in cases where boys can't seem to centre themselves as comfortably as girls, they might need other means of releasing excess energy.

- Enjoy your time with your baby, toddler or young son by not worrying about whether they're missing out on anything by not having Dad around. At the same time, don't avoid 'Daddy stuff' totally. It's OK to read stories about all kinds of families to your child. Place a high value on male and female relationships in order to give your child a realistic perspective.

- It's easy for mothers to think of nice things to do with their daughters, but sons and their male interests can be more foreign to us. So set aside some quality time to spend with your son doing 'male' things like watching a sport, going to a museum about something he's interested in, etc.

> ❝ Fatherhood after divorce comes easily as long as you put the children first. Demi and I are friends, I think we have both chosen to rise above what you commonly see when parents separate. It is simple, really: we both love our kids and want to raise them together. ❞
> Bruce Willis

Chapter 8

MONEY MATTERS

Like any decent balance sheet, this chapter will focus on the ins and outs. Fear not, it's not all pound shops and market stalls and it doesn't mean the days of M&S and designer jeans are completely gone. Because we're going to show you not only how to spend more wisely but also how to kick-start your brain into thinking about making some more money.

First off, we want to get money into perspective so that you don't let money, or the lack of it, control you. We advocate getting a vice-like grip on your finances. It's guaranteed that this will make you feel better. We will also try and open up your mind to getting creative, getting out there and getting earning. We're total believers in the goal of financial independence.

From a financial point of view, becoming (and being) a single parent can be extremely daunting. It could be that you haven't been involved in the pounds-and-pence part of life before, or it may be that you find yourself with zilch, or a lump of wonga that you don't know what to do with. Whatever your situation, it's highly likely that, however much you had before, you now have less at your disposal. On top of this it probably feels that the responsibility of managing the household finances as well as everything else is just one more thing for you to do and can be the straw that breaks the camel's back. All in all, money can easily become an albatross around your neck.

The Emotion of Money

Nothing brings out emotion like the topic of money. In a world where people bare all manner of private details about themselves, their lives, views and habits, money is still a sensitive taboo subject. Maybe it's because it's seen as a measurable degree of success or failure that's best kept under wraps. Or that jealousy, envy and bragging are unattractive traits.

Although maybe deep down we know that money can't buy contentment and it feels that all manner of learned folk continually bombard us with the notion that personal happiness is not linked to money, for those struggling and finding themselves in a financially constrained position, having more money can seem like the answer to so many problems.

So once and for all, let's put money into perspective and never forget that even though the best things in life really are free, being able to enjoy life without financial worry is well and truly worth the effort.

That said, we do just want to plant the seed that, since time began, and in most civilizations, there's been a perceived order about what we as individuals are trying to achieve. Here's the order of what we strive for – you'll see that you only need money for the first, most fundamental one.

1st need	Enough money to take care of physical needs such as heat and food, clothes and a place to live
2nd need	To be loved and relate to others, to value ourselves, have friendships and love
3rd need	To leave a legacy, to have a sense of purpose and to make a personal contribution. In a nutshell: to leave the world a better place. A big part of that for parents is to do your utmost to bring up well-balanced, good and valued members of society.

So when you're contemplating everyone else's apparent wealth and how green-eyed and unsettled it makes you feel, remember that you only need to be sure you've got enough money to cover your family's physical needs. The other stuff you can still achieve without money. So do the best you can with what you've got and then, once you're making the most of your assets, start to think about increasing the amount coming in.

Single Parents and Money

Once separated, the average single mother sees her income fall. It can feel that the whole financial thing is unfair, particularly when your ex appears to have a better quality of life than you. He may tip up to see the children in the latest designer labels while you're kitted out from head to toe in stuff you've had for ages. On the positive side, keeping up with the Joneses is so far off your radar that this is no longer an issue. Hurrah! This is a good thing, as you can gather inner poise from realizing what ridiculous and petty games most people play competing with friends and acquaintances about possessions and brands.

Money, Power and Control

Apart from bringing up the children, money may now be the only current connection you have with their dad. Because of this it may be that negotiations and conversations with each other about money are really about so much more. We don't intend to sound flippant, but we bet this sounds a bit familiar, we've all heard it said, or thought to ourselves: 'Why shouldn't he pay for his children? He can afford it. Why should I cope with less?' There's no mention of 'need'. It's all about exorcising the hurt and anger left over from the separation. Money is such a powerful tool and can become about more than what we need – it becomes about power and control. We believe that the best way to handle this is to try and neutralize it as a weapon by working towards financial independence.

Dear Kate and Emily,

My husband and I have a daughter and separated about 18 months ago. All was going as well as could be expected to start with: our daughter saw her dad at weekends, we didn't have to leave the family home or move her school as we both have good jobs, so money wasn't a problem. It was when we started to sort out the divorce that it all went wrong. My husband refused to pay any maintenance as he argued I earned more than enough to live on! I couldn't believe he'd be so selfish and tight-fisted. It's academic how much I earn, as our daughter has a right to some money from him too, especially if he wants the right to be her father. I'm fighting him in the courts on her behalf, and when she's 18 I'll show her all the legal papers that have accrued over this battle to show her how hard I've fought for her and how little he really thinks of her. Then the scales will fall from her eyes and she'll know the truth.

Love,

Court Battle of Chelsea

Dear Court Battle,

You mean to say that you and your husband are both sufficiently wealthy to give your daughter two homes and a stable environment, and that as a separated couple you were able to get on well enough for your daughter to have a relationship with both of you, and yet you're fighting in court? Get in your daughter's shoes and ask yourself if she'd rather have harmony or battling parents and no relationship with her dad plus a carrier bag full of legal papers that prove no more than your ability to be so blinkered you can't see how poorly the whole sad episode reflects back on you.

Neither of us can ever imagine being told what you're planning on telling your daughter at 18 and throwing our arms gratefully round our mum's neck and thanking her for all she did and for

showing us what a low-life our dad is. Can you?
Get a grip, Kate and Emily

Money and access have nothing to do with each other

We want to make it clear that we believe that money and access to the children are *not* linked in any way whatsoever. This may seem a really bitter pill to swallow: 'Why should someone who refuses to pay be allowed to see their child?' We want to show you that access to the children and receipt of money for their upbringing should be kept *entirely separate*. If their dad isn't contributing properly on a financial basis, and is therefore shirking his *financial* responsibility, this shouldn't have any bearing on his relationship with the children. This must be dealt with as a separate issue.

This is a really hard one. It feels wrong, it feels unfair and it feels so out of order. Well, it does at least until you turn the issue on its head and realize that, although you're punishing Dad by withholding access to the children and getting the demented loony reaction that you wanted from him, MAKE NO MISTAKE: you're also punishing the children and maybe even more than him. The children cannot be the ones made to pay for this situation. Keep it away from the children and know that one day when they're old enough to work it out they'll realize the extent of your sacrifice and magnanimous attitude.

If your ex won't pay or is unreliable

Don't

- burden the children, however old or wise you think they are.
- withhold access to the children or use the children as pawns in any other way.
- use the children as messengers, sending them in knackered old clothes or using any other subtle (!) way you think will get the money message across to their dad.

Do
- go through the correct legal channels to sort out money. If you still hit a brick wall, we say, very unfashionably, think of yourself and your children and don't spoil your life with an ongoing battle that will stop you moving on.
- appeal to their dad's better nature. The best way to get the money out of someone is to make them realize that it's the *right* thing to do. Most people try to do the right thing.
- rant, rave, swear and throw things generally or carry on in an open space or down the garden shed; BUT ONLY when the children are elsewhere!
- let it go. You know it's an outrage, you know you're right.

Although you may be screaming and shouting about the injustice, it's still your battle and not the children's. They'll work it all out for themselves one day; so in the meantime let them get on with their childhood. Their dad may be unreasonable and unfair, but until the children are old enough you don't want them to realize this because:

- It'll upset their relationship with their dad and affect their self-esteem.
- They may start to believe that this is OK behaviour, and you certainly don't want them to grow up with a warped value system.
- They don't need to carry the burden that would surely be on their shoulders if they realized fully that their dad was making life very difficult for you.

Moving on
Let's work towards 'Financial Goddess' status.

We really want you to work towards getting into a position of strength where you know what you have and what you need, where you have developed your own good monetary habits and are happy with the goal of financial independence. There are numerous reasons why, but the main ones are:

- This will do wonders for your self-esteem.
- You'll be able to move on as an independent woman.
- It will challenge and develop you.
- It will stand you in good stead for the rest of your life.
- Your work ethic will be providing your children with a great role model.
- You'll be encouraging your children to have a positive attitude to money (passing on money-management tips is a great way to help your children).
- It will give you back control of your life.

We're not suggesting you turn into Nicola Horlick (or some such superwoman juggling being a single mum and super City high-flying success), but that you always think about money in a positive and constructive way and get control of the whole business.

Knowing where to start, what to do and how to grab the bull by the horns can be overwhelming, but fear not, be brave. Once you're off the starting blocks it'll be a truly positive and liberating experience. If you can do basic maths or work a calculator, you're more than capable of making some marvellous inroads into understanding and managing your financial future.

Once you learn to take care of your finances, you'll never look back. The confidence and purpose that you get from growing financial empowerment are tremendous. Managing your money is not rocket science and is an area of your life that can turn from an albatross round your neck into something positive relatively easily. Getting to grips with your finances can not only be fun (?!), it's also immensely rewarding to see the pounds go further and, absolutely best of all, it gives you back a feeling of control and really helps with moving on.

Who Are We to Talk?

Kate says
Strangely enough, this is an area where I can speak with some vague

authority as I've got a finance degree and a postgraduate qualification in investment analysis. As well as passing my exams I also spent over ten years of my professional life as a financial manager. I was, though I say so myself, pretty successful (this is not as a brag, though I'm clearly being unattractively immodest, but in an attempt to inspire confidence!) (Oh, reaaally??! Love, Em xx)

Know the Detail

Having run money I know that things go wrong when you take your eye off the ball. I also know that credit card, mortgage and utility companies rely on customers being sloppy and abnormally loyal. It all adds up to the dead certain knowledge that ostrich-like behaviour costs money.

Avoid Taking Risks by Mistake

Ignoring problems can be very expensive (for example, going overdrawn on your current account without making an agreement). Don't waste money insuring yourself against risks that you can afford to take (like buying a warranty for a camera) while ignoring those risks that would really knock you off course (such as ignoring the consequences if you become too ill to work). It means paying bills on time, or paying by direct debit if it's cheaper. It also means starting to save even a small amount every month (regardless of how little you have), and if you've debt coming out of your ears, getting it all together and starting a repayment plan to get out of the hole. Another negative consequence of not thinking ahead is that when something which could have been reasonably anticipated happens, you throw money at the problem (for example, having to get your engine practically rebuilt because you didn't check the oil level regularly).

Get the Best Value for Your Money

Chez moi, when I became a single parent I hadn't paid any bills for five years despite having been an independent girl about town. On marriage I turned into a financial passenger! I hadn't done a bean with the bills, car tax or MoT (I didn't even fill the car up with petrol!); in fact, I hadn't done anything. I was just given money at the end of every month to pay for food and clothing. Exit husband, and I was amazed by how much money went out: council tax, water rates, phone, TV, insurance, etc. Every month there seemed to be 'something' I had to pay. I realized pretty quickly that I had to stop writing cheques and taking money out of the hole in the wall like a headless chicken and start using my noodle. Never in a month of Sundays would I have behaved like this at work. No, I would have made clear, sensible decisions based on value, having shopped around and considered the options.

I soon realized that the lessons I had learned at work could be applied to my finances at home. It didn't take long, but it did require me to get my head out of the sand.

Emily says

Money and I have had an interesting relationship, to say the least! When I was at college my dad used to forward my bank statements to me with 'SWALK' (sealed with a loving kiss!) written on the back, and really they were – it was the good old days of knowing your bank manager, of having a nice man on your side who would smooth over things with his colleagues and waive the overdraft charges. Money was never scary: I might not have had much of it, but I knew some-one sensible was looking after me. Then there was my husband, who was fantastically sensible and wise about it all and kept us living with-in our means and saving money. He shopped around for deals and was generally on top of it all. So I never really thought about money.

After we split up there was only me in charge, and my favourite phrase is, 'When you're out, you're out' (i.e. if you've bothered to go out for an evening, shopping trip, weekend away, etc. don't scrimp – you're out to play!). Fortunately I'm not that daft and I knew that I had less in the pot than I did when I was married; the problem is that the rocket-scientist part of me is my most boring side, which I usually choose to ignore in favour of the happy-go-lucky part of me.

I thought I was cutting down, but was always amazed when my bank statement showed how I'd failed to reduce my spending. It wasn't a major situation; it was just that over the years the overdraft and credit card bills were slowly building up. Then I had three realizations that led to my financial rebirth:

1. Every month I had something out of the ordinary to buy or pay for (ranging from Christmas to car tax). I realized there is no such thing as a 'usual' month, so time to stop pretending my over-spending was just a series of one-offs.
2. There were no obvious expenses I could cut out: no expensive habits or excessive lifestyle choices.
3. It was OK to sometimes say 'No, can't do that, sorry' to mates organizing a night on the tiles, etc.

Then I had a bit of a tearful session with the old girl (Kate) when all my well-buried/ignored worries about my money came flooding out (literally).

It was time to take Kate's advice, so I did all of the stuff she's written up for you later in this chapter, including the spending diary (she says it's fun to do – it's not, but it's necessary!). I'm self-employed, so my finances can vary a bit, so knowing more about what I've got and being more aware of what I'm spending has meant that I now live within my means even though my income hasn't changed.

My top tip would be: every payday, take off the amount you know will be going out that month – include all standing orders and known one-offs – then divide what's left by four and take that much out in cash each week, and don't touch your plastic. This focuses the mind and all your spending decisions!

Try not to be too drastic, though, because the chances are you'll find it hard to stick to your resolutions and will give up. Be realistic when you think about changing your financial habits and developing new ones. As time goes by you'll become increasingly savvy. It's very like going to the gym: a bit of a pain to get started, but once you see the benefit it can really make you feel better and more in control.

And we're off ...

Taking Charge of Your Finances

By adopting habits that you're comfortable with, you can manage to have a better attitude to money (this isn't going to turn a generous soul into a mean one, just into a more careful one). So try not to see dealing with money matters as a punishment but as a means of dealing with those things that you always meant to deal with, and of developing a system and a lifestyle that suit you.

Kate, for example, is not planning to start taking flasks of coffee out with her as she loves a good latte (extra shot), nor planning on turning the heating off and going to bed in a bobble hat. But she does know that there are lots of ways she could save money:

> I had the wrong mobile contract and I saved money by changing utility provider. I know I should shop around and stop buying clothes that are too small (despite being tremendous bargains!), plan menus and eat foods that are in season. These are just a few of many changes that won't alter the way I live but they will reduce my spending and I can easily do them.

Five Easy Steps to Becoming Financially Fit

Here are our five easy steps for you to follow in a way that is manageable and that you feel confident you can stick to.

1. *Go on a fact-finding mission* – Be crystal clear about where you are NOW.
2. *File or pile* (depending on whether you're a filer or a piler) – Write down all the financial commitments that you have (or anticipate having) across the year.

3. *Read the numbers* – When you know how much money you're likely to have, make it work sensibly but as hard as it can, every single pound. Know where it's coming from and where it's going.

4. *Financial goals* – Know what gives you the willies, calculate which risks you're prepared to take and those that you're not, and then manage the situation.

5. *Hi ho, hi ho, it's off to work we go.* If you're feeling like Grumpy, get into the Happy mindset of trying to bring more money in (don't be Dopey). Sometimes people need a little push as they can't get their head around how, so it's easier to stay as they are. But hey, some day you're going to have to deal with this, so start to push yourself out of your comfort zone and look at the world of work – you'll feel more relaxed and in control once you have.

Step 1 – Go on a fact-finding mission

Establishing an operating budget is important. To do this you need to know how much money you owe and how much you've got coming in, as well as how much you're spending. This critical step is often ignored because it's hard to dare to see how little you have and how much you owe. This is advance preparation, so put a date in your diary for two weeks from now when you'll really start the regime. In the meantime you're on a fact-finding mission as part of the all-important 'knowing where the heck I am NOW' phase of the exercise.

You Will Need
- a shoebox
- an exercise book
- a calculator.

Over the next two weeks you'll be creating a spending diary, gathering information and (if you can't find bills) contacting your bank, utility providers and anyone else to get the information you need about your accounts.

Gather everything: long-forgotten building society accounts, premium bonds, every store card you've ever opened, child benefit, tax credits, income statements, National Savings and records of any debts that you have. As you do this, put everything you find in your shoebox.

Next, write down all the bills that you have to pay over the whole year; try to find old examples of these and shove them in the shoebox too.

You can use the 'shoebox technique' forever, putting anything money-related in it and dealing with the contents once a month. Make a diary note each month to deal with the box. Get your bank statement to come monthly or, for enhanced monitoring, bank on the Internet.

Now start a spending diary. For two weeks, write down everything that you spend (from a book of stamps to parking meters to clothes and food) in the exercise book.

Having done all of this you'll be armed with all the information you need. It doesn't matter that you haven't looked at the statements or even opened the envelopes. That can be done in Step 2!

Step 2 – File or pile

It's money night ... come on down, 'The Price is Right!' Two weeks after Step 1, it's time to sort the information you've collected into four piles:

Pile 1 What's Coming In?
Evidence of any income or money coming into the household:
- income, anything at all
- tax credits
- maintenance.

Pile 2 What Are You Spending?
- Bills (having found or requested your last bill for all regular outgoings) including rent/mortgage, water/gas/electricity/TV plan/council tax/mobile phone/car insurance/household insurance, etc.
- Day-to-day expenditure as noted in the spending diary.

Pile 3 *What Do You Owe?*

- Credit cards, store cards, bank accounts, loans, mortgages, etc.
- In your spending diary make a note of all payment dates, APRs (the annual percentage rate, a standardized way of stating the total cost of a loan. It takes into account the interest rate, the timing of the interest payments, the timing of capital repayment, other charges and arrangement fees). You don't have to know how to work it out, but know that one APR can be compared with another.

Pile 4 *What Have You Saved?*

Any assets that you have:
- savings accounts
- National Savings
- house
- premium bonds
- other.

These piles need homes and can't be left as precarious mountains of paperwork all over your home. Having all your financial information in one place is important. Although Kate reckons the world is made up of filers or pilers (she'd be a piler), if you can find another way of keeping this information together and in one place, then great.

In your spending diary, using a page for each month of the year, note down the expenditures that occur only at certain times of the year (TV licences, birthdays, Christmas, car insurance, holidays and so on).

Step 3 – Read the numbers

Examine the piles and go through each item to see if the position could be improved. If it could, set yourself a target for improving it next month. 'Pile examination' (of the financial not medical sort!) will occur on a monthly basis and you'll come to enjoy the feeling that these sessions give you. They'll help you see how much you really need, and identify where you're spending more than necessary on things that aren't really important. This is what you're looking for as you go through the four piles or files.

Then read the numbers, add up all your sources of income from the 'What's Coming In?' and 'What Have You Saved?' piles, and then look carefully at the 'What Are You Spending?' pile.

Looking at What You're Spending

For each bill, really look and think if there's a better way, and do you really need this? Kate, for one, has just abandoned digital TV as 'there's plenty enough on the channels you get free with the TV licence for me, and with the money I save I can virtually take out as many DVDs as I can watch.' But maybe it would make sense to get a Freeview box? Then ring up each provider and ask the straight question: 'I'm looking to reduce my bills, but before I do a proper price comparison check and decide, can you let me know the best tariff you can offer me? Is there a way that I don't know about that could reduce my bills?' Once you've done that, check out the competition. The easiest way to do this is to use a price-comparison website. Something else to consider is whether direct debits would suit your style or finances better, as quite often suppliers will give you a financial incentive to pay by direct debit, and there's better scope to plan.

Having looked at your regular outgoings, take a long hard look at your everyday spending in order to fill out the budget schedule below. Complete it for one month and see if there are any spending areas that you'd like to set a target to reduce, then go for it. For the next month, set yourself a little game to see how cheaply you can live without changing your lifestyle. Using the budget schedule you might see what you can change, and by how much, each month. Write a list of how you might do this that fits in with how you want to live. Kate's might include some of the following:

- menu-planning and then buying only for what I've planned, so I don't waste food

- sorting out my mobile bill
- getting my utilities on to direct debit
- buying children's presents more cannily
- seeking entertainment at the library or all the free museums around
- going to the Vidal Sassoon school for a good cheap hairdo.

At the end of the month of trying a new budget and saving money, analyse the data. There could be as much as a 20% improvement on some categories. From this, establish some good habits and develop some savvy financial-wellbeing routines so that you know what you're doing, where, why and at what cost. Then take a little time each month to keep on top, review, monitor and act.

Review your Piles

Look at the pile of what you owe, and find out the best way of servicing such a debt. So, say you've a total of £20,000 debt. Take time to find out the cheapest and best way of paying this back. Go to your bank and ask them what sort of a loan they could offer, compare rates with other providers, go to the Citizens Advice Bureau and ask them, or call the debt service advice line and talk to someone about it. Bet your bottom dollar you'll not only find a cheaper way of servicing the debt, but also a manageable and achievable way out of what can be a very worrying financial hole. Do make sure you get *all* your debt out there and covered with a manageable loan, then chop up your store cards and credit cards.

At the end of this step you'll have the basic financial statements that will tell you where you are NOW. Having looked at them, you'll see where you're going and what you can change, as well as spotting the numbers that look out of kilter (10% of your income going out on the TV is out of kilter!). The general idea is that Pile 1 and Pile 2 should match, and Pile 3 and Pile 4 should balance. Maybe they don't now, but that's what you're working towards.

Personal Budget Calculator – Monthly Expenditure

	Current spend (£)	What can I change?	Target spend (£)
Fixed expenditures			
Mortgage/rent			
Council tax			
Water rates			
Gas			
Electricity			
Telephone land line			
Telephone mobile			
Home insurance			
Home maintenance			
Children's education/uniform etc.			
Life insurance/pension			
Loan repayments			
TV/internet			
Variable expenditures			
Petrol/travel			
Car maintenance (service, MoT, tax)			
Food and non-alcoholic drinks			
Household goods			
Medicine/toiletries			
Hairdressing			
Personal items – self			
Personal items – children			
Clothing and footwear – self			
Clothing and footwear – children			
Holiday fund			
Leisure/going out (including babysitters)			
Other			

Dear Kate and Emily,
I've never done the money. It was a 1950s-style marriage and he did everything. I didn't even know which bank we used. All the post was addressed to him. I'd only ever open catalogues to flick through and all the rest I left to him. This has been the worst bit about him going. You see, I think I've enough money because he tells me it's all paid out automatically by the bank and he's giving me more than enough to cover it all, or so he says. I haven't opened anything for nine months and nothing's gone wrong … so far. I'm so scared and don't know where to start. It's making me ill and taking the shine off my penchant for champagne and facials.
Love,
Money Worries of Monaco

Dear Money Worries,
Thank you for your letter. Your story shows how you don't actually have to be poor in order to feel the debilitating worry that goes with it. However, poor or not, you must take action. Get a trusted friend round for a confidential post-opening session. It'll probably take a full day, but needs to be done. As you go, sort it into piles according to the sender and then, of course, a pile for junk mail. Put all your statements and bills in separate piles in date order so you can trace what's happened and assess what's owed, what you spend, and what you've got. Together, work out what your monthly income and outgoings are and come up with a budget for you to follow. You may find that cheaper champagne (served with a white napkin wrapped round the bottle to fool guests) is in order. But equally, you may find that all is as your ex says and a celebratory facial is called for! Either way, you absolutely must find out what state your finances are in and understand them.
Love, Kate and Emily

Our Top Tips for Staying on Top of Your Money
- Every few months, write everything down that you spend in one week. Everything. It helps to stop bad habits resurfacing!
- Surround yourself by positive people/make a new financial buddy.
- Develop goals that fit in with your values.
- When bills and financial statements come in, pile or file them and review the whole thing once a month so you keep this little baby under control. It'll get easier and quicker every time.
- Spend cash only.
- Reduce your number of credit cards to one and use it carefully and infrequently.
- Never spend more than £75 without a 24-hour cooling-off period (abandon impulse purchases).
- Don't leave electrical items on standby; it means they're still using electricity. Turn the heating down a degree or two and buy energy-saving lightbulbs. Going green and being more aware of your carbon footprint saves money as well as the planet!
- Increase your financial awareness by reading the money pages in the paper or watching the business programmes on TV. This will demystify a simple subject and make you feel more financially confident.
- Spontaneously plan. Take advantage of promotional gimmicks so you go to the cinema on the cheap night, and take popcorn you've bought in the supermarket, etc.
- It can feel like purgatory scrimping and saving all of the time – if you're saving for something special (a holiday, a new sofa, a groovy pair of shoes), put a picture of it on your fridge. It makes it all feel worth it and is something to look forward to.

Step 4 – Financial goals

Having looked at your current position and immediate budgeting plans, now it's really useful to take some time to think about the future. Write down financial goals and make them as specific and measurable as possible. At the outset, try and think of small, short-term and realistic ones, though working towards some long-term dreams and the elimination of some long-term niggles is also a good idea. Note down the things you want to achieve and also your worries about getting these addressed. If you can, prioritize them and try to break them down into short-, medium- and long-term goals. Don't believe that your goals are unobtainable just because you can't reach them now.

Long-term goals might cover areas such as:

- buying the house
- holidays
- education
- retirement
- a savings pot
- private healthcare.

Writing goals down helps you to focus, particularly with regard to increasing the income levels coming into the house. If you can make them even more specific, so much the better; for example:

- *I want to stop living from month to month. I would love to have a rainy-day pot of £250.*
- *I would like to take the children camping next year and need an extra £500 by next July.*
- *I would like to pay the mortgage off in 10 years' time.*
- *If I become ill I would like to know that I could afford to live.*
- *I need to earn an extra £50 a month.*
- *I want to be able to afford to send the children to university.*
- *What's going to happen to me when I'm old? I've no pension arranged.*

Think about these issues realistically and ask yourself:

- How hard are you willing to work towards these goals?
- How will you feel when you find yourself working towards them?
- Are your goals driven by factors such as security, freedom, choice and time to do what you want, such as being with the children? They should be!

Focusing not just on what your goals are, but why you want to attain them (e.g. to feel more secure about your future or to have the freedom to make your own choices) makes the whole business so much easier because the emotional reasons underpinning your goals are SO worth working towards.

Bravo, you've established an operating budget as well as understanding your financial situation, and you're working towards improving it all in both the short and long term. Now for making money!

Step 5 – Going back to work

Returning to work after a break is a daunting experience for many mothers, let alone single ones who have to manage work and home on their tod and who often feel very under-confident. It doesn't make much difference if you're going back to work because you're bored at home, miss the 'adult world' or because you're strapped for cash and need the income – whatever the motivation, you're bound to be anxious about it. Many of us have worried about what to wear, being too rusty and out of date to use the computer and printer, let alone understand what the hell our colleagues are talking about! And of course – will you be taken seriously? Can you really do this? It's pretty likely that post-divorce you're going to be relatively low on the old self-confidence, so pushing yourself onto the job market can be one problem (or 'opportunity', as work would have us call it) too many!

If this is you, and you're full of self-doubt, then at this stage it's important to say that working is a doddle compared to bringing up a young family. If someone in HR were to write a 'person specification' for a stay-at-home parent, they'd find no candidate who could conceivably be all the things that you are: good communicator, problem solver, juggler, teacher and trainer, counsellor, negotiator, financial planner and, of course, in possession of fantastic time-management skills and never crumbling under pressure (especially if there's a large glass of wine to hand!).

Writing Your CV

Before you begin your return to work, it may be worth writing down what your experiences have taught you and how you can turn these qualities into skills that would make any prospective employer put your CV at the top of the pile. Writing your CV is the most important process to securing your interview. A CV, like a person, is judged within the first five seconds. It's worth spending some time making your CV do you justice. The layout should be clear, modern, professional and straightforward. Don't try and be clever with different fonts and flowery language.

Here are some general tips, though it would really be worth a visit to the library and a good browse in a book specifically covering this topic. Even if you think you've nothing to write down, take a pen and paper and make yourself write down your best traits and skills and the things that you're most proud of achieving, and make sure the flavour of these permeates your CV.

CV Top Tips

- Keep your CV to two pages, max.
- Do your CV in reverse chronological order. The recruiter will want to find the most relevant part of your CV quickly, which is normally your last full-time job.
- Be really careful with spelling and grammar; poor speling and, grammar, can loose you the inerview (oops!).
- Remember transferable skills that you've gained since you last worked and try and fit them into your CV.

- Make sure your CV is relevant to the job you're applying for. If you're applying for a PA position and your last position was a film producer, highlight the similarities of the two roles. This is true when relating all the skills you as a mother bring to the party, be they organizational skills, party planning, fundraising for local toddler groups or schools, or keeping your cool when everything's falling apart.
- However well someone's skills fit with a prospective employer, if they can't work as part of a team and lack social and life skills, they won't get the job. Most employers are interested in who we are as people, not just what we do. They can always teach someone.

Once you have written your CV it may become obvious to you that you need to refresh your old skills or even learn a few new tricks. This is the point before you actually bring the CV to life and boost those areas by seeing what your local authority has on offer and taking a few courses, or getting more active in your community, campaigning for more playgrounds, etc.

Don't be too complacent, though. We would recommend refreshing your IT skills so you at least feel confident sending and receiving emails, using the Internet and Word, etc.

Places to Look for Jobs
- Websites – from virtual recruitment agencies to your industry association's website sometimes posting vacancies
- Trade/professional magazines
- 'Staff Wanted' signs in windows
- Think laterally and work your way up – if you want to work in the school office but there's no vacancy, take the job as playground assistant. At the very least you'll be on site and will have the advantage of being someone they know when the job you do want comes up.

Top tips for those already in work

If you're already working, then please take a few minutes out of the general hurly-burly to read through these bullet points to get you thinking around and reviewing yourself and your work. The MoT in Chapter 3 (Looking After You) also has a work section that we strongly recommend you read. But for now:

- Know your worth. If you think you deserve a pay rise – ask.
- Take control of your career and your life.
- Would a challenge energize you? Is it time to push yourself out of your comfort zone and go for a promotion or new role?
- If you don't like your job, or feel undervalued, look for another.
- Think about starting a business or making money from home.
- Is going freelance/part-time or doing flexible work a possibility or even an attractive idea?
- Keep up to date by taking up any training opportunities.
- Write your CV, spot the weaknesses and improve it where you can by gaining the relevant experience. Keep it current. Power to the people and all that.

Think about the following questions; they might ignite some ideas for you:

- What do I enjoy so much I would do it for free?
- What do other people tell me I'm good at?

Money-making wheezes

Not all of these are entirely sensible, or even things that we'd be prepared to do for money! However, they do get you thinking out of the box when it comes to generating a bit of extra, or a steady income. Use them as inspiration.

Life Model

If you're up for a bit of public nudity and don't fidget, then you can earn over a tenner an hour as a nude life-class model. Apparently models are in demand, so call your local art college or find a local 'life-drawing' class and ask if they need anyone!

Dog-walking

How hard can it be? Other than leads getting tangled, forgetting Rover's name as he runs off, and having to bag shed-loads of poop. Apart from that, if you're a doggy sort and like a walk you can walk a dog for about an hour (or less) and earn a fiver – get several dogs and it's not a bad earner. Ask at your local vets, put ads up locally and see if there's a local dog-walking agency in your area.

Host Foreign Students

Contact local language schools and find out about their host-family programme. The more you host, in terms of meals provided, the more you're paid. Not a bad earner, and if that feels too daunting and you're not sure your house is up to scratch for paying guests, then how about doing what Emily does, which is host a foreign student in return for childcare and housework?

Interviewing

This one had to go in as Emily's a market researcher! How about being an interviewer who goes door-knocking? Travel time, petrol and a fee for each interview is usually paid and can add up to a fair bit. It's a popular job with women who want to be home-based and work around their family commitments. Or, of course, telephone interviewing if you'd rather be based in a telephone centre and talking over the phone. Then there's mystery shopping, which is pretending to be a 'normal customer' and assessing the service, etc. you get and feeding it all back to the research agency. Contact the Market Research Society for details of agencies.

Babysitting

OK, rubbish if you don't have child-free nights, but if you have and you're strapped for cash, what could be easier than babysitting for over £5 an hour and a taxi home if you don't drive or want to drink? (Joke!)

Quizzes
Sign up for TV quizzes, do the rounds of pub quizzes and take part in competitions. Warning, though: this could become a rather worrying addiction.

eBay
This requires a bit of time to visit the site and work out how to use it properly, plus a digital camera for taking photos of your wares. You really will be making money out of nothing; some people have even made trading on eBay their full-time job.

In the Wee Small Hours of the Night

At the beginning of this chapter we talked about not only knowing where money was coming from and going to, but also the importance of being careful about the things that could go wrong. Making sure that you've thought carefully about these things and taken steps to cover these risks makes financial sense and also gives you peace of mind – and the effect of reducing worries and niggles can be considerable.

Having control of your money on a day-to-day basis is liberating, but it's also necessary to think about the bigger picture and the 'What if?' scenarios. What ifs are those scenarios that could knock you off course, making things really difficult for you, and what we want you to do is to think if you could make life easier for yourself and reduce your worry levels by being prepared and having them 'covered' should they ever occur.

It could be that some of the issues listed here are niggling you, or you may have other worries pertinent to your own situation. This list isn't finite; it's merely a selection of gremlins that we find come up time and time again. Writing down your concerns may just make you think, 'Yes, I need to get that worry sorted,' for example appointing a guardian and writing a will should you die, or simply just talking about your options further. If this is the case, then you may need to seek advice from friends and family, or if they don't have any experience of it, then a solicitor or an Independent Financial Advisor (IFA).

'What if?' scenarios to think through

- *Mortgages*. What if rates go up and I can't afford my mortgage? Do I have the best mortgage? What's a divorcee mortgage? What happens if the economic climate changes and we get back to high inflation, high interest rates? Can I protect myself?
- *Illness and death*. What if I become ill? What if their dad loses his job? What if he becomes critically ill? What if he dies? What if I die? Who'll look after the children if we both die? Who do I want to look after my affairs if I'm too ill or die?
- *Pensions*. Who's going to pay for my retirement? What pension provision do I get from the government? Do I get a pension from anywhere else? How much will I need?
- *Savings*. How can I start saving? I really want to get into the habit; can I start factoring a small amount into my budget?
- *Taxation*. What do I pay? Do I need to submit tax returns? Have I been putting enough aside? Am I in trouble if a tax demand plops on the doorstep? Do I know about, and claim for, everything I'm eligible for? Do I need an accountant or to speak to the tax office?
- *Debt*. Is my debt making me nervous? Have I lost the plot as to how much I owe? Have I worked out how I'm going to get out of a huge debt hole?

All of these are things you need to think about, work out what you want, and perhaps discuss with an IFA – or at the very least with someone like your parents, brothers, sisters, friends who have done some of this before.

IFAs: Who they are and what they do

An Independent Financial Advisor (IFA) will go through your finances, assess your attitude to risk, work out a financial plan to suit you and source the best-value products on the market.

Most banks and building societies offer their customers financial advice for free, but the difference is that such advice is not independent: they will sell only their own products, which may not be best suited to your needs and situation.

IFAs may give you the heebies and you may worry that their advice will cost a lot, that they're sharks and will be trying to sell you financial products you don't want or need. This really shouldn't be the case, but you should choose your IFA with care.

As with everything from plumbers to hairdressers, a word-of-mouth recommendation is worth its weight in gold, so ask around. However, if one isn't forthcoming, the next step is to visit the IFA Promotion's website. Enter your criteria and postcode and they will give you a list of the IFAs that best suit your needs in your local area. You can ask for a free consultation with the ones you like the look of before choosing which to go with.

Before you take on an IFA, remember to ask about the level of qualifications they hold. As with most things in life, the more the merrier! All IFAs are required by the FSA to have a Financial Planning Certificate (FPC). Ask if they have an Advanced Financial Planning Certificate (AFPC) or if they're an Associate of the Society of Financial Advisers (ASFA). If you require specialist advice (on pensions, tax issues or investments, for example) you'll need an IFA with additional qualifications. The IFAP website carries a list of the qualifications you should look out for. However, no matter how many qualifications your IFA may have, you must feel confident that you can trust their advice. If you don't feel entirely comfortable, then this IFA is probably not the one for you.

If you do end up having a problem with your IFA, you do have methods of comeback. First, be sure that your complaint is reasonable. IFAs can be held responsible for bad advice or mis-selling, but not for the poor performance of products that they recommended to you in good faith.

How to Pay an IFA

Always ask an IFA how they charge. IFAs charge in one of two different ways: through commission or with an upfront fee. If you choose a commission-based IFA, you may not pay anything upfront at all, but he or she will be paid commission on the products you buy. Fee-charging IFAs, on the other hand, will ask for an hourly fee.

Although the idea of avoiding a one-off fee is appealing, questions have been raised over whether IFAs who charge commission are always entirely independent: the temptation to recommend the products that pay the highest commission may be there. For this reason, the FSA is advocating a general move towards fee-charging rather than commission-based advice.

How to Get the Most out of Your Session with the IFA

To avoid paying an IFA to sort your piles out, attend the session with everything in order so that you can get the most out of the time. It's worth taking recent bank statements with you, your total income for the last three years (and any proof you might have, like a P45, or your accounts), good estimates of your outgoings, etc. so they can see how much money you've got to spend on a pension, mortgage, etc., whatever it is you're talking to them about.

Once you've established your operating budget and can articulate your concerns about the bigger picture, an IFA will have a very clear idea and be able to offer relevant, good and useful advice quickly.

> " After the divorce, I didn't want to just sit around and shop and spend my ex-husband's money ... I wanted to 'transform' into someone else. It was just a way of getting away. And I can see that the acting came along at a time when, having been with Mick so long, I was very unhappy, feeling trapped, afraid. Afraid to stay, afraid to leave. It's another transformation. "
> Jerry Hall, *Independent* 27th August 2001

Chapter 9

OLD LIVES, NEW LIVES

You're waving goodbye to the traditional way of doing things and your life has become unscripted. One day this uncertainty, which can feel very scary, won't seem so bad after all. It'll dawn on you that new horizons are emerging. You've got a fresh start; but don't leave all your old friends and ways behind you. Instead, it's time to keep the stability of the old and refresh them with the thrill of the new. Nervous? We're not surprised, but we'll help you to rebalance your life, shifting its focus from the old to the new. This could be a laugh, couldn't it? A brand-new life, a change, a challenge and an adventure? Maybe you're through the woods, the children are past the nappy phase and now out in the big wide world. Start thinking about the future when it's YOU time. You've probably noticed the change already ... once the pain and the aggro begin to settle down and you've begun to stabilize your ship, you can have a fresh start – and not only that ... life can be very, very good.

There are lots of contradictions involved in single parenting, with feelings such as isolation and contentment, euphoria and misery happening simultaneously.

One of the first things we do when we get a new group of single parents together is to take some time out to jot down on pieces of paper:

- things that are worse now
- things that are better
- things that are just plain different.

We then take the middle pile and think exclusively about the parts of life that seem better as a single parent. Focusing on those for a moment, most groups we've run end up with a very similar list for that middle group. People scream out their thoughts, often hooting with laughter, recognizing themselves, agreeing and so on. The list tends to look pretty much like this:

- I am no longer seen as wife/mother but seen as me.
- I don't know what's round the corner and it's so exciting.
- Married people's social lives revolve around dinner parties; thank goodness I don't have to go to *those* any more.
- Married people have to compromise; it's liberating to have total control over domestic circumstances.
- Life seems to be more spontaneous and varied.
- I don't have to see my husband's friends – I never really got on with them.
- I don't feel bound by convention and am no longer part of social competitiveness; it all seems too pathetic from here.
- Child-free weekends give me space and time to pursue all sort of things I wouldn't have been able to do without them.
- I don't have to have sex when I don't really want to (or with someone I don't really want to bounce around with!).

All theses things are ace, which can be a bit of a double-edged sword and an unspoken *niggle* to those still in the rough and tumble of married life. Well over half the single parents we've come across have expressed intense disappointment and surprise over the way their married friends have behaved. This has not only been about how girl-friends have reacted but can be even more acute when you find that couples' attitudes towards you appear to have changed quite radically. Men may feel threatened as they see their wife's friend turning into a new giggly girly larking with their wife and regaling her with tales of life on the 'outside'. They have probably been very patient and now fear that their wife might be tempted even for a nanosecond! Even though the thought of luring his wife into the world of singledom is no more likely than looking for a love interest from within the married scene, it's clearly true that you may make even dear friends feel uncomfortable.

As a wise old bird says,

> 'I think a single woman is always seen as a threat and I sometimes wonder if people think of divorce as 'catching'. I feel so disappointed I just want to shout out, 'Please include me just like before'. Yes, I like your husbands but I haven't changed into a predatory woman overnight. Besides, not one of them would attract me out of a burning building – even if he were single – so please, trust me, your marriage is safe!'
> A Single Mum

Even though it's likely to be true, it would clearly be rude to make your position so obvious by suggesting that they had unfanciable husbands!

As we've found friends to be an important issue, we've included a big chunk devoted to them before we think about all the lovely bits and bobs that can spin out of this new, unscripted and unexpected change in your life.

Friends

Friends are generally highly rated by Kate and Emily. They are a fabulous source of fun, laughter, chat and company, and really make you feel as though someone is on your side and looking out for you.

The sisterhood can be the best thing in the world. But before we get carried away, don't forget that some girls can also be a bit on the gossipy side, loving nothing more than to chew over the bones of a good tale. Often they're so fascinated by what has happened to your marriage that they can end up making you talk about it loads and encouraging you to stay in the victim/bastard stage for longer than you need to. Don't get drawn into dissection if you don't want to.

If your friends are anything like Kate's they'll support you in their own way. When she was first left they all behaved differently. One spent hours talking, planning and advising, another just offered lots of childcare, tea and sympathy, and Gill took her to the Malvern House parents golf dinner in a large borrowed dress and some flat shoes to get her out of herself!

But do tread carefully, don't overestimate and overburden friends; they're also human with their own lives, ups, downs and other relationships. They'll listen to you, they'll support you, they'll take care of you – but as with all relationships, there needs to be give and take and you must take care not to overdo it by becoming self-obsessed, boring and static. Of course we all go through needy patches, but make sure friendships remain balanced and just remain aware of the length of time that you might be in the needy phase. After a period of time when you feel up to it, make sure you do a bit of rebalancing, though not in the 'Enough about me, let's talk about you. What do *you* think about me?' kind of way!

One of the people we know does a lot of charity work as it means that people get to see her in a different light rather than being just 'Sarah, the one Andrew left'. It means she has conversations with people about events, etc. where she's an equal player. She's a good example of someone who has managed to get more of a balance in her social life.

However, there are times when we do need to talk 'single parenting' stuff. This is where we've found that talking to someone who's been there makes all the difference. Friends and family are just as likely to over-react as under-react, thinking things are worse, or better, than they are: often they just don't get it. We MASSIVELY recommend that you get a group of like-minded single parents together. You'll build a group of friends to talk single parenting to, and you'll be building new friendships with people who understand where you're at.

We're afraid to be the bearers of bad news (if you haven't already found it out for yourself) but: your couple friends may stop inviting you to things and you'll drop off their radar. What makes this bad news is that it happens at a point in your life when you're already feeling a bit useless, rejected, failed, washed-up and unpopular because you've been dumped/have dumped. Let your Billy-no-mates mantra be, 'It's not me that makes them flee, I'm just single and hard to mingle. Must pick up the phone and invite them to my home.' Repeat this to yourself and you'll begin to feel a bit less sensitive about it. Remember that your couple friends won't be missing company in quite the same way as you. That means they just won't be in touch much – that's *normal* for couples. Your singleness will make you extremely aware of how infrequent it is, and as you're feeling low you'll think it's all about you. It's not! Be realistic about friends. Your social scene WILL, without a doubt, change. So what do you do?

Your old friends

You've got your own old friends, the ones that you've known since primary school, college, first flat share, etc. These are your friends and they'll stay that way, probably because they knew you first as plain old Jane, before there was ever a sniff of Peter, so you no longer being Peter-and-Jane doesn't throw them quite so much.

It's also loads easier for old friends not to feel as if they're caught between a rock and a hard place trying to decide whose side to take. Actually we're putting a huge caveat on this – you won't lose any of your old friends just because you're separated, but you might if you behave poorly – but that's up to you.

Dear Kate and Emily,
You say get in touch with old friends. Well, I can't. My best
friend has a lovely house, a double wardrobe stuffed full of
gorgeous clothes, a charming husband and a happy life – all
because she married a good one and I married a bad one. I can't
bear to see it or to be reminded of how far I've fallen.
Love,
Green with Envy of Grantham

Dear Green with Envy,
You're talking about your BEST friend! Surely if places were
reversed you'd still want to be her friend? And miss her enormously
if she avoided you. How about meeting up somewhere neutral like
a wine bar so you don't have to see her home? Don't allow yourself to be isolated, or surrounded only by people you think are
worse off than you. Seeing real, old, good friends is a true tonic.
If you insist on being eaten up by jealousy, then you'll send your
friends running for the hills, and then you really will be in trouble.
Who cares if you can't afford to ski? What has that got to do with
being a friend? Stop trying to keep up materially and just be yourself. Trust me, that will be more than enough for true friends.
Good luck, Kate and Emily

Spontaneous planning

You need friends, so don't be ostrich-like about this. We all get amazingly
used to our own company, and get to the point where a night in front
of the telly has more appeal than a night in front of a real live person!
When you get to that stage, though, you've got to take yourself in
hand. Emily was one of these people full of promises of action who
wanted to rock-climb, host soirees and so on, full of ideas let down

by inertia at the point of execution. Then watching a friend at work planning his diary she had a eureka moment, for this chap was doing what he called 'spontaneous planning'. His spontaneous planning involved about five minutes of frenzied activity as, having spotted an advert for a show, he'd spontaneously called the box office and bought two tickets for months in advance (that's the planning bit), knowing that he'd be able to find a friend to go with, with that much notice. It was an inspirational moment and now Emily has at last spontaneously planned getting old friends round on a regular basis. *(Oh yeah?! Are you just not inviting me? Mind you, there was that great time when you booked tickets to watch the bearded blokes doing ballet – Kate)*

Entertaining

Kate has a revolting phrase – 'kitchen suppers' – which she uses to describe what she's invited friends to. It means she's just feeding them pretty much what the children are having, or what she would have been having if no one had been coming round: expect cold mini-pizzas and garlic bread lightly tossed in an enormous bowl of salad (true!). Let's hope you enjoy it if you ever have the good fortune to be invited to one of these 'events'. *(Dear Emily, That was **not** a 'kitchen supper'; that was when you came round for a drink, had had no supper, and I cleverly whipped up a snack for you from the leftovers to soak up the wine. No, Kate's Kitchen Suppers are a one-pot, tasty yet wholesome, easy-to-prepare-in-advance meal, to be enjoyed round the kitchen table with a minimum of fuss. Love, Kate xx)*

What you call these evenings doesn't really matter; the most important thing is to not get in a tizz about it, because simplicity and cutting catering corners are done in order to maximize your enjoyment, and enjoyment is key! Happy host, happy guests …?

No Excuses

Although there are a million reasons for *not* getting people round, most of these don't stand up under scrutiny:

- Cost? You can do a kitchen supper for £1 a person – bit basic, but possible.
- Time? You're in, so what else are you up to?
- Busy? What with? Urgent need to catch up on the soaps?
- Tired? If you don't make a meal of it, it need not be too much work – and a good evening can be *soooo* energizing.

Last top tip is that it's much less stressful having several people round than just one or two. This is because you can spread the jobs out among your friends, and also if your children do call you upstairs you can attend to them without feeling too bad leaving your guests on their own. It's amazing how much knowing that relaxes you.

That's enough on entertaining and keeping your social network going – neither of us is marvellous at it, but what *stops* us from doing it is usually apathy (which we hate in others), procrastination (which is Emily's middle name) and a feeling that it's all a bit more bother than it's worth – which is totally untrue, as those evenings always leave you feeling beamy afterwards. It's just a matter of starting.

Now on with all the best bits of unscripted life – read on …

Your Future

Change will happen, it is great to have thought about it, to be prepared for it and to have a plan, even if those plans change. It helps us to embrace the future and make the most of life. But facing uncharted waters, dreaming new dreams and hatching new plans can be difficult and daunting. These are the things you need to mull over.

For most folk, thinking about what to do with your life can be alarming – maybe that's why so many of us avoid thinking about it. It's important to allow yourself time before you can move on. Set yourself some long-term goals and start working towards them. It may sound a bit daunting, but writing down goals may help to sharpen up your commitment, resolve and motivation.

The future depends on the choices you make. Taking the bull by the horns requires a certain amount of risk-taking and commitment. Here are some top tips to nudge you into really thinking about the future:

- Make an effort to get out of your comfort zone. Have something written down that is challenging and gives you the collywobbles.
- One of the by-products of this is that you suddenly see the world in a new light, which is wonderful.
- Get out of the *que sera sera* way of thinking. Stop thinking it's not worth planning.
- Become more proactive and know that YOU make things happen. Good things happen as a result of taking action.
- Take a good and realistic look at your family and see how it will change.

Step 1 – How is your situation going to change?

Begin to imagine the future: which bits of your life are going to change? Some might be changing just as a result of time passing (like the children growing up); other changes might be inflicted upon you as a result of your separation (like the need to move out of the family pile); others might be changes that you want to happen (like getting a new job).

This is how Jane divided up the changes that she imagines will be happening to her in the next two years. Do the same for yours.

Changes that just will happen	Changes that I've got to accept but don't like	Changes I want to happen
The twins Dotty and Spotty will be at secondary school. The twins will be much more independent and get themselves to school and back. They'll get more expensive.	I'll need to earn more money. I'll have time to work more. We will need to move to save money.	I'll have time to do a photography course. Dating......!! Time to think about me more! We'll have moved nearer my family.

Step 2 – Know exactly what you're aiming at

Once you've done this, write down some concrete goals and a plan of action. Get giddy at this point, as you've really committed to yourself and this feels like it's actually going to happen.

Goal	Action
To take a photography course	Do some research to find out which course I would like to take. I may have to save for it.
Dating	Find a local speed-dating evening. Set myself a start date in the future. Get myself match-fit; trawl the Internet for a bloke I like the look of.

Step 3 – Make it happen

This is where things get a bit military-like. Top-notch planning is called for. Look at your own chart of the things that are inevitably going to happen, and think through how you're going to make sure your changes happen without catching you unawares. So, for example, if Dotty's a one for charging over roads without looking and her iPod on full whack, then between then and now you've got to make sure she's learned how to cross roads safely so she can get herself from A to B.

Or 'They'll get more expensive' – a much more daunting prospect, but calm yourself, it hasn't happened yet and you've done that amazingly sensible, grown-up thing of thinking ahead and planning for it! So, any chance of saving even a fiver a week? That'd be at least £500 you'd have up your sleeve after less than two years, which must help calm that panicky feeling. The idea is that by looking just two years ahead (which isn't far), you can take just very little steps to make sure it all happens in a way that you can handle. Bite-sized pieces, ladies, bite-sized pieces!

As for the changes you can't wait for to happen (for example Jane's dream of bouncing around the boudoir in something frilly), it still needs planning and thinking about, not rushing in, all guns blazing! All changes need a bit of thinking through.

Emily says:

> I have to have a plan in my head, which says this is where I'm aiming for and this is how I can get there. My current plan is to make my bathroom look like something out of an interiors catalogue. How? Thank you for buying this book! I'm saving up for it, and know that by next year it'll be a bathroom to be proud of. Next plan may feature a bevy of handsome devils in my new bath!

One of the most alarming things about becoming a single parent is the billion-and-one decisions that have to be made, from the very mundane like 'Shall I put a wash on tonight?' to the massive 'I'll let the spare room to a lodger.' To some people decision making is second nature and doesn't throw them at all; to others of us, at first it's something that we have to do, then when we get the hang of it our idea of a dream holiday is not to have to make one single decision! Imagine how fantastic it'd be to be told where you're going, what you'll be doing, whom you're meeting up with and, to top it all, having someone else choose from the menu for you, order drinks for you … a heavenly holiday for a week, after which you'd probably be itching to be back in the driving seat!

For those who haven't yet got the decision-making knack, here are some things to ask yourself. These questions act as a useful second pair of eyes on the situation. You see, that's what many of us are missing – someone else to bounce our ideas and plans off. Consider these questions your decision-making other half, as they're designed to force you to examine things and to think realistically before you act:

- Can I afford to do this (in terms of time/energy/other resources)?
- Is the upside large enough to outweigh the downside?

- What's the risk? Is this plan more likely to fail or succeed? Why?
- Does this plan really fit in with what I believe in and how I want to live my life?
- What problems will this change create in terms of friends and family (especially the children)?

If you can answer these questions positively, and feel forewarned of the pitfalls you'll meet on the way, then you're on the way to making decisions that will be good for you and your family.

Step 4 – Keeping the children onside

These changes are things that we know we're going to have to facilitate or avoid. However, our children are not necessarily involved in this process – though they will obviously be affected by it. How to introduce the change to them, and lead them through, will be vital to the success of your dreams for you and your family.

Did you *really* think through the question:

- What problems will this change create in terms of the children?

OK, you have now. You know it's not plain sailing, but you know why you're doing it. The secret to successfully helping children through change is to **talk, talk, talk, and take your time**. Never assume that children are fine with everything because they haven't said anything to you. *Ask* them, and ask them in a very neutral, non-committal way so they don't feel any pressure to agree with you and so they feel happy telling you if something does worry them about the change. Then you can deal with their worries.

> After the divorce my great fear was: I've never had to do anything for myself. With Mick it was all chauffeurs and bodyguards. But last week I took the train from London to Cardiff on my own. I even went to the snack bar and had some awful coffee. I was so proud of myself.
> Jerry Hall, © *Guardian News and Media Ltd*, 2007

Chapter 10

DATING

Even though you realize by now that relationships don't always run smoothly, the prospect of a new 'special person' is a lovely thought and truly evidence of hope over experience. The daydream of a new romance, a bloke with a rose between his teeth and love in his eyes, is something to look forward to. As Kate's very happily married sister said in a bit of a jealous way, 'Ooh, you're going to fall in love and have a first kiss again!' Well, yes! Now *there's* something to keep you going.

However – and there always seem to be 'howevers' in this book – the thought of starting a new relationship can be quite simply terrifying. We know that this whole subject can potentially be the most challenging of the lot. Especially as when you start to think about new relationships you can worry about things related to yourself (like your confidence) as well as how the children will be affected and the effect their presence will have on the course of true love.

Over the rest of this chapter we will boost your confidence by getting you to think positively and help you to get going on the dating front by giving you some ideas (some more sensible than others!). We're a bit on the lighthearted side because we think this is an area where you can get out, have some fun and mingle – and if you can't feel light-hearted about the whole thing, then stay away from potential targets until you've got a smile on your face and a bit of a spring in your step. The challenging part of dating comes when you've actually found someone, at which point there does need to be delicate handling. We suggest keeping the children out of the picture completely until you feel that a relationship has a future.

When your romance becomes more serious, some planning, thought and preparation are a very good idea. Remember that many relationships fail where children are involved. This is often because, in a haze of romance and 'lurve', you think it's so great that everyone (children included) will be tickled pink. This is one of the many mistakes Kate made: when she had a serious romance she didn't give enough (any!) thought or time to integrating everyone involved. She was like a bull in a china shop in a haze of giggles, kitten-heeled mules and lipstick. Who knows what might have been had she been more sensible rather than going for the ostrich-like 'If I am happy, so are they' attitude?

So we're here to provide a degree of perspective, confidence and practical advice on getting, introducing and keeping new partners. The dos and don'ts (pages 225-226) are top tips gleaned from our and others' bitter experience of mucking up new relationships while the children became unpleasant and anxious! Even if you haven't yet nabbed a new partner, they're still worth a quick look.

Dating and new partners

Our pearls of wisdom on this subject, it has to be said, come about as a result of having made a huge Horlicks of the whole thing while observing the success stories of others. As they say, 'There's no one better to ask directions than the person coming back the other way' (although in our case empty-handed!).

Where are we now? Well, Kate had The Big Romance. Two years after divorcing her husband, a friend and neighbour invited Kate for dinner. *Whoosh,* she fell hook, line and sinker for the lovely Jimbo, a childless divorcee who was very funny, nice, sociable and tidy. They say opposites attract – in this case perhaps only on the tidiness front! It was a heady period for Kate and he moved in with the gang and found space for his trouser press among her chaotic piles just months later. The pace was fast and furious because, as Kate says, 'I was sure I would marry him and live happily ever after and the children would totally adapt. I was thinking lots of laughing and fun like in *The Partridge Family*.' Then the happy couple and children went on holiday to Portugal. This was like no 'holiday' Jimbo had ever been on before. Holidays with small children are different from grown-up ones; it's all sun hats, factor 50, making sure they don't drown, and finding food they'll eat. This was not the holiday the lovely Jimbo had in mind! He beat an early retreat! Back at home the chaos the children created narked him. Returning from work in the evening he would get changed and be ready for a chilled glass of wine and a chat while Kate wanted to finish the homework off and flop in front of *Coronation Street*. After a while Kate realized that she couldn't keep everyone happy and pretend the children didn't make the most almighty difference to spontaneity, privacy and everything else. Her daughter, meantime, was beginning to be horrible to the lovely chap. Not so she could be told off, but enough to be subtly pushing him out. Kate describes how it all felt:

> I felt as though no one was happy and I was caught in the middle, so I'm afraid I gave up. He's still my friend, but I am going to wait until I've real 'me' time to fully enjoy a romance. I totally believe that the prospect of love and romance is out there for everyone, whatever age, type or size you may be or the baggage (or small valise) you carry with you.

So currently Kate is in the 'It's not worth the aggro' camp. Maybe writing and reading this will let rip and spur her on to have another go, having thought about it properly. We will keep you posted.

Emily, on the other hand, has seen less action since her marriage ended, with the exception of one incident which Kate feels 100% sure she won't wish to share with you, dear reader. However, at this point in time Emily's very much in the 'I feel ready to find someone to care about me and have some fun with in my child-free time' camp. So she has set off on a mission, and as such has more tales to tell from the field.

Are you ready to date?

As you go through the process of adjusting to being on your own as well as devoting time to settling your family, you may find that you just don't have the time or energy to start to think about new partners. On top of this, the end of one relationship can be emotionally draining and, now you're through that particular wood, thinking about commitment may be the last thing on your mind. These are good reasons to wait until you feel more yourself before you launch into the arena. That said, you may badly need a boost to your confidence, crave some male company or just simply feel crap being single – all good reasons to join the dating game, but words of caution: try not to confuse being lonely and miserable with wanting to have a boyfriend.

If you're feeling a little low and down, rather than setting yourself up for disappointment and disaster, give yourself the best possible chance. Get to know yourself and get comfortable in your skin. I think we all sort of know that the best time to seek is when you've lots to share and feel comfortable, relaxed and content. Let's face it, if you're needy, miserable and feeling low in confidence, you're not likely to attract much, no offence. Don't be bullied or pushed by friends or relatives keen to see you 'sorted', or even spurred on by the most natural desire in the world to prove to yourself (and anyone else who may see you in an unattractive light) that you're indeed still desirable. Wait until you feel ready in yourself to play the dating game. So rather than dive into a relationship that you're not ready for, hang fire on the actual dating process and prepare yourself for the day when it does all start to happen. Remember, relationships built when you're feeling needy and vulnerable might be on shaky foundations.

However, if you feel low and dating or going on the pull cheers you up, then go and dip your toe in, or have a full-on skinny dip in the pool. We pass no judgement on those who like to bounce around on a Saturday night with a hot date. We simply say steer clear of trying to find, develop or maintain a relationship if you're not happy within yourself.

Being bashful types, we won't dwell much on sex, but maybe your marriage wasn't satisfactory *au boudoir*, or never fully functioned, so you see being single again as a great chance to upgrade your sex life. Or perhaps you miss the closeness of intimate 'relations' despite whatever else was going on. Sex is a funny old activity, and as a friend once said to us, 'When you're down it's like the most amazing cocktail of intimacy, making you feel wanted and desired – it can be such a quick fix.' It is a quick fix, though, not a proper watertight solution. No, even though you may miss sex and all that goes with it, do think before leaping into the action.

What do we need relationships for?
We get different things from different types of relationships, be they friendships, family or of the romantic variety. There's a difference, obviously, between all of them, and we need some of each type in our lives. All of these relationship types need some maintenance. Thinking of all your relationships, identify the different types (friendship, family, romantic) you have and see if one or two types might be missing. The point is to help you aim for a bit of a balance.

As far as relationships go, there are four basic needs that we're looking to be fulfilled:

1. emotional
2. spiritual
3. intellectual
4. physical.

Although friends, family, colleagues and other people can fill the top three of these, they're unlikely to manage to succeed with the physical one!

If you don't feel ready to date but miss the physical thing, then let's think about other ways of filling the gap created until you're feeling ready for more. Many of these suggestions are aimed at helping you to develop some creativity. Even if it's not something that has appealed to you in the past, we urge you to try and find some creative outlet. We've heard time and time again that boosting your creative juices is the most successful way of filling the gaps that a lack of lust and 'lurve' creates. Here are Kate's tips to get your creative juices flowing:

- Write. Writing is like a muscle: the more you do it, the more you enjoy it (as the actress said to the bishop!) and the better you become and a whole great virtuous circle has begun. Write letters to friends, write a diary, write to the papers, write short stories, a book or a screenplay. Or just take an A4 lined exercise book and every day fill a page with ideas, lists, things you need to do and things you would like to find out about.
- Paint and draw. If you've a poor imagination, start by sketching a vase of flowers, trees, the children, or copying a photograph you like. Then get a 'How to' book out of the library.
- Create collages, cutting and pasting things that you find attractive or want to remember into a scrapbook. Our favourite involves getting a load of travel brochures from a travel agent and thinking about where we would like to go one day.
- Take up a musical instrument. If the children are learning, then try and teach yourself while they're not using it. What fun to be able to play the oboe, organ or recorder, or take a dance class, learn circus skills … for example.
- Get crafty! I am going to put this even though I know Emily will howl. Knitting, tapestry and embroidery, all very creative and therapeutic.
- Find an amateur dramatics group or join a choir. Or just sing like a loony at any opportunity you can find.

Dipping your toe in

There will come a point when you feel that you do want to start going out and meeting new people, as you're beginning to feel like your old self. It could be you don't want to 'go steady' but you do want to go out and have a look at the talent. This is a great attitude and a fab way to start. Don't confuse dating with going husband-hunting, though. You may want a serious relationship, but be careful not to skate over the period in the middle when you're playing the dating game again. All the minefields are still out there just as they were when you were in the arena last time around: there are the cads, the fly-by-nights, the great pretenders and the teases. If you've the right attitude, then you can enjoy being out and feel able to cope with the odd knock to your confidence, and the odd encounter with a cad.

Top Tip 1
Remember you're going out for a laugh, company, a flirt and a nice time. If you think in terms of 'meal ticket', 'new father for the children', 'security' or 'someone to look after me', then just watch out. You may send them running for the hills and set yourself up for disappointment.

Top Tip 2
Have fun! Treat nights out as time for yourself (it's not the time to talk about the children and how hard the nits are proving to shift). This is time just for you to be frivolous. At this point this dating lark has zippo to do with the children. Think back to the attitude that you had in your late teens and pre-serious relationship stage. Dating then was just that, i.e. going out on dates, having fun and having someone to knock about with, so relax about it all. Did Kate go out with Charles Jarvis in her teens because he would make a good husband? Did she heck; it was his Doc Martins that did it!

Top Tip 3
Don't obsess about how you look. It's wrong to think you have to be perfect before you date. So if you feel ready to go, don't put it off, believing that you must shift that extra stone before you launch forth.

What are you after?

Having thought about whether you're ready to date, now think exactly what it is you're after from the dating game. Here are some things that others have told us:

- *'I miss sex and physical contact. I want some between-the-sheets action.'*
- *'I want someone to look after me and care for me.'*
- *'I want someone to take me out and make a real fuss of me on my birthday.'*
- *'When I got to the point when I felt like the Big Brother house-mates were my friends, I knew I had to get out more and literally "get real"! I wasn't going to meet someone at home.'*
- *'I don't want anything more than company.'*
- *'I want to have what everyone else has.'*
- *'I want someone who's as interested in me as I am in them.'*
- *'I've just got rid of one man, the last thing I want or need is another, but someone to buy me dinner every now and then would be nice.'*

So what do YOU want?

This may help you to work things out:

Go into fantasy-land, cutting and sticking to your heart's content. Be as imaginative and freewheeling as you fancy – cut out pictures, parts of pictures, words, colours and shapes. Build up a collage that describes your dreamboat (don't forget to include the flaws you're prepared to handle!). Once armed with your dreamboat spec, you're focused and sorted!

Are the children ready?

The immediate thought that might pop into your mind is, 'Are the children *ever* ready?' On the one hand they want you to be happy, and are more than likely to thrive and benefit when you are. But on the other hand they're unlikely to want to share your time and attention. It's probably unlikely that you'll hit on a serious relationship straight away, so it's sensible to keep transient relationships away from the children. Being ready and enjoying the freedom to explore single life is ace, but our view is that introducing the children to a range of folk is far from ideal. We say keep the children out of it until the relationship has gone up a notch or two. In fact, as a rule of thumb always keep your children's involvement one step behind your own.

As we know, children aren't mad keen on change and are very 'me me me' focused. The thought of you with a new partner may well be one change too many. They'll quickly and correctly realize that you having a new partner will lead to less attention and time for them. The last thing you want is for them to equate less time with less love. They may well view your boyfriend as a replacement for their dad, and that could mean the beginning of the hard realization that Mum and Dad really aren't going to get back together, which is a fantasy that many/most/all children have in some shape or form.

Just as *you* need time to readjust to being on your own again, so too do the children. We advocate giving dating a miss until you're through the difficult parts of separation, as that will give the children time and space to adjust, too. This should probably be no less than a year; Kate waited two years until she waded in and broke all the rules to her cost, and Emily is yet to wade anywhere, but that's more a function of circumstance and opportunity (or supply and demand!) rather than careful planning. She reckons, like Kate, that after a couple of years it would have been, in theory, OK for her and the children if she'd dated.

Think ahead and start laying the groundwork. Defuse problems that might happen with lots of preparation. The idea is to provide heaps of subtle, good and positive messages around the whole subject. Let the children know that although it's quite normal for children to want their parents back together, this is not going to happen. Make sure your children understand this before any new person/partner rocks up onto the scene and gets all the blame for destroying this fantasy. You can also lay the foundations by:

- talking about the possibility of new and special people in the future, hypothetically.
- helping your children to understand the difference between romantic love and the love and joy they bring you. This will help avoid the fear they may have when you do find someone that they're not enough to keep you happy.
- focusing on building strong relationships with the children that can weather the change.
- meeting and mingling with other families where new partners have been successfully integrated.
- stressing that any new partner won't alter Dad's relationship with the children.
- rooting out positive films and TV programmes where the subject is happily incorporated.
- stopping bed-sharing NOW and introducing some concept of privacy.
- setting out some time that you spend out of the house with friends developing your social network. This'll show the children that you need adult friends in the same way that they need their friends. When you're ready to become involved with someone, there'll be more of a natural transition as your going-out habits will already have been set.
- skating around the topic gently, introducing and talking about it in a non-threatening and positive way.

Dating as a Single Parent

Dating as a single parent is not massively different to dating as a non-parent. However, it's understandable that you may feel less confident and gung-ho than you did in your younger days – and to be honest, things are slightly different, but lots of it's just in your head:

- Maybe you feel you're starting a little bit on the back foot having lived through a failed relationship.
- Maybe you feel that you're past your prime.

- Maybe you feel that your beloved children will be seen as baggage.
- Maybe you have a negative view of the pool of potential Prince Charmings.
- Maybe you just can't see anyone and, rather than face disappointment and another disaster, you decide literally to stick to your knitting.

Try and look at all of these concerns from a slightly different perspective:

- The fact that you find yourself in this position, reading this book, is just one of the consequences of the rich tapestry of life. You know deep in your heart of hearts that it doesn't mean you're too fat, boring, useless and/or uninteresting. It means that your relationship didn't work. Although this is a part of your history, hopefully you've well and truly parked it and won't want to go on too much about it when you're out and about on the pull!
- Past your prime?! That is all in the mind! There's someone for everyone, but if you know that you'd feel better in yourself if you took some more exercise, or shifted a bit of weight, then do it. If you want to ring the changes with a new coiffure and feel that would boost your confidence, then do it. Love and romance are about sparkle and attraction at lots of different levels, and we're sure that by the time you're ready to date you'll have realized that you're pretty fantastic!
- As a wise friend/romantic interest of Kate's said, 'It's obvious. Most of the best women have been married and had children by the time they get to your age.' That felt nice and true and, instead of making Kate feel old and past it, she felt like one of the best now back on the market. Yes, the children can make things slightly less spontaneous and different, but they're part of your package and anyone who has a problem with that is just not a runner.
- There are potential partners out there for everyone. They just haven't made themselves known to you yet! Which might be because you're scaring them off by looking all grumpy with a

'What's the point?' look on your face. Or you might be surrounded by your friends so they can't get to you, or maybe
you're just not meeting enough new people. Or, most heinous of
all crimes, you've discarded someone immediately because they
didn't tick enough boxes on your rather inflexible list! Keep an
open mind: he may be in the beer garden reading *The Real Ale
Lover's Guide* and wearing a pair of grey shoes, so what?
Abandon the list, don't expect a potential suitor to come in the
size and style you ordered. Relax, open your mind and give Mr
Grey Shoes another 15 minutes of your time, order a cheeky half
of ale and then decide!
• Didn't Oscar Wilde, the master at keeping his pecker up in the
face of adversity, say something about true love being the triumph of
hope over experience? Keep plugging at it ...

Starting to date again
Now that you're in the right frame of mind and feel ready to date, let's
see how best to go about it.

Looking the Part
When preparing for your date, think how you're perceived by the outside world and about what you want to say about yourself – does it
match what your appearance is currently saying? Contrary to popular
belief, and despite the fact that Kate looks like a bag of old spanners
much of the time, there's nothing superficial about appearances. They
say a lot about who you are and, importantly, how you see yourself.

Take a look at successful TV personality and single parent Carol
Vorderman. She's changed her look from mumsy academic to raunchy
siren, a change that coincided with weight loss and the end of her
marriage. Her new outward appearance reflects some big changes.
Maybe you weren't thinking of raunchy siren, but do think how you
would like to be perceived.

What would we do for a bit of a brush-up? We'd probably:

- shift that bit of weight
- have a good session in the bathroom with a lady Bic
- get up the hairdresser's for a new coiffure; if broke, volunteer as model for FINAL year students (last thing your confidence needs is a beginner hacking at your hair).
- sort out the wardrobe and select the gear we feel good in
- invite a friend over who knows about make-up, and have a make-up session.

Sharpening Your Social Skills

Have you got out of the habit of meeting new people and talking to men? This can make many people feel like giving up, as the thought of having a conversation makes them feel uncomfortable. They don't know what to talk about and are tongue-tied at the mere thought of it all.

This is Emily's strength to such an extent that she has little idea of the difference between talking to her friends, the children, work-mates, the pet rabbit or a man. As a consequence the men get thrilled and believe that as a result of their magnetic chemistry they're in with a chance, when nothing could be further from the truth as she talks to everyone in the same lovely, caring, relaxed way. Although this has landed her in a bit of hot water, and led to a few awkward situations, Kate seems to think that we could all learn something from Emily's communication techniques. *(Emily would like to add that this is Kate's take on things, as it has passed Emily by – which probably proves Kate's point about how she should be a bit more careful about the way she talks to blokes!)*

Emily's Communication Tips

- Smile a lot and laugh at all their jokes.
- Aim to bring a smile to their face (even parking attendants).
- Have an interesting nugget up your sleeve that you've noticed in the paper or on the telly.
- Ask questions in a non-interrogating style, e.g. 'The last CD I

bought was *Music to March to* by the Royal Navy Regimental Brass Band. I've got it on my iPod and march everywhere blowing my imaginary French horn! What was the last CD you bought?' It's a gentler approach than an interview-style 'Where do you see yourself in five years' time and how to you hope to achieve this?'

- 'If money were no object, what would be your ideal mini-break?' Get some dreams, hopes and aspirational chat going. If the person you're talking to doesn't have much to say about their life (or it's boring to listen to), then getting them talking about hypothetical things can open up a rich seam.

- Seek advice on a subject you'd like to talk about, e.g. 'I need to get a new TV, do you know much about them?' So even if he bores the pants off you, at least you'll have found out the answer to a question.

- Always have one very pathetic joke up your sleeve! Preferably not along the lines of an anecdote about your children: 'Oooh, you'll never guess what little George said last week!' More along the lines of, 'What did the 0 say to the 8? Nice belt!' – gets them every time and gives them *carte blanche* to tell you theirs (which you laugh at) and they feel like a fabulous entertainer and the life and soul of the party.

Value Yourself and Meet Lots of People

This is the type of ghastly step that one reads from time to time in books that reckon there are 'rules' to follow if you want to nab a man. Underneath it, though, there's a simple message that's worth considering: Don't make yourself too easy, don't chase, don't accept anyone just because they've got a pulse, and don't put up with something not very good. But DO put yourself in situations where you meet and get exposed to lots of new and different people (men in particular), DO abandon preconceived ideas and just meet, meet and mingle. This is, after all, a numbers game. The more people you come into contact with, the more likely a suitable and lovely partner is going to appear on your radar screen.

When you've met someone you like (assuming he likes you), there's nothing that will get in his way or put him off trying to get to know you better, children and all. This is because you're great, amazing and have a rapport with him that doesn't come along every day. It's true, but you'll still need to be helpful and encouraging, because even the most ardent of flames can be put out with too much coolness and too many brush-offs.

Where do I start?

Without further ado: into the *piscine* ... The plan is to put yourself in as many situations where you can cross paths with other people as possible. Remember that everyone has family, friends, neighbours and colleagues. The more people you mix with, the more potential suitors you're likely to encounter.

Golden Rule

Don't discard people too quickly. Stick at it. Don't decide to rock up at the book club held in your local library, have a look round at the load of old grannies and think, 'Not for me.' You may enjoy it anyway, and who knows? People can spin out of the most unlikely new contacts. Think laterally: grannies have sons, friends and neighbours!

Here are some ideas of places and ways to meet new people. Some of the ideas will just widen your social circle and get you in touch with more people, others are more obviously singles-focused. We've bickered a bit about the order, as we wanted to rank them from least frightening to the 'Whey-hey, I'm up for anything' end of the spectrum – only to discover that we've different ideas of 'Whey-hey'! Anyway, the order's not important – read them all and try the ones that appeal to you.

1 Make New Friends

This is the greatest way to extend your social circle; in fact it *is* extending your social circle. Write a list of people you'd like to get to know better. Then ask a group round for a very casual bowl of pasta and salad, or suggest going for a coffee. Also, make contact with people you've lost touch with.

2 Network

Here's another phrase we believe: 'The more you give, the more you get.' Join in like fury, so if you're ever asked to help, try to say 'Yes,' be it at the school, in a neighbourhood watch group, at the church, at the children's football club, fundraising. All these things will bring you into contact with more people you have something in common with.

3 Join Something that Fits in with Your Spare Time/Child-free Time

- Pilates/yoga (nothing like chatting to a new friend with your legs round your ears, and unable to hold farts in)
- Join the WI
- Film club at the local cinema
- Rambling group
- Netball team
- Amateur dramatics
- Political party
- Conservation group
- Choir
- Contact a local charity and volunteer
- Local libraries often run book clubs, and in addition have files and details of many local clubs and organizations.

4 Take a Course

There's a wealth of courses run by the local education gang, some in the evenings, some during the day. Maybe this is something you could consider for your child-free time. Kate trained as an aromatherapist, loved it, met lots of completely different people and acquired a skill that she could turn into a money-spinner. She was watching a flower demo at a country show recently and thought what a lovely craft it was and one that could be turned into an income stream. Other things she'd like to learn about include photography, painting and writing (probably not best to confess to that here). Emily would like to sign up to do a beekeeping course, wine appreciation, French, Spanish and tennis courses. Create your own list, and make the most of the Internet to find out what's available in your area – then get involved.

5 Work

Why not think about killing several birds with one stone and getting a job? This is truly a great way to get to know people better. We've put this in just to nudge you to think about *all* the ways that you can get new people into your life. And as, after the age of 25, over two-thirds meet their partners at work, it doesn't sound such a daft idea. This should be seen as yet another good reason for getting a job. Bit of a mad idea: why not get a babysitter and find a job in a nice wine bar one night a week?

6 Tell Your Friends

Friends have popped up in several sections of this book. We've found that they're extremely important, but we've also learned that they don't always know what to do for the best. They may feel so unsure about what to do about including you in social functions and worry you might be upset. Will you feel like a spare part? What if they invite you with someone and you think you've been set up? As a result, what tends to happen is that friends end up taking the easy way out and just not inviting you to anything other than lunches or girly suppers. It's up to you to remind them you're around and fun and on for being set up! So take the bull by the horns and let them know that you'd love to be included in mixed company and that you really don't mind being the odd number, that bowling up on your own doesn't bother you and that you most certainly don't mind being fixed up – in fact, the more match-making they can muster up, the better! If they say, 'Oh, Johnny's great fun but I don't think you'll fancy him,' say, 'Hey, who cares? I might, and if not, the more single friends I have, the better.' A good way to actually get this ball rolling is to host the very type of event you'd like to be included in, with couples and singles – the whole shooting match. That said, we do think that a rather blunt spreading of the word to your good friends is the order of the day.

7   *Speed-dating*

Despite the fact that neither of us has ever done speed-dating, we think it such a great idea that we've often included it in the prescription we write when people are wanting to kick-start their social/romantic life. We've had many great reports back from the melee. The reason is simple: it gets you used to talking to lots of new people for just a few minutes a go, which can be fun and gets you into the whole swing of practising conversation with a single man. It may sound on the con-trived side, but it's easy to get tongue-tied and practice is great. One of the tales that came out of our TV series was a really lovely girl we sent speed-dating. She had a fun evening and, although she didn't meet anyone that night, she felt so liberated by the experience of being able to have fun talking and chatting that when someone who'd caught her eye in the past smiled at her on the train, rather than bury her head in a book she was able to engage in a chat. Her radar had been retuned to 'receive and give messages'. Getting your radar working is half the battle anyway! So go for it, find a friend to go with. It's organized and hosted, so you won't be left floundering. Don't be dis-appointed if you don't hook up with someone; just know that it's a really useful exercise in getting you into the swing and limbered up.

8   *Internet Dating*

This is more Emily's department, the lovely Kate being far too shy to meet some complete and utter stranger in a bar. That said, we've heard more good reports than bad about Internet dating. There are sites that match single parents together, so that might be worth con-sidering, though there are loads of divorcees with children on most of the sites. Obviously in these cases all participants have a good under-standing of the whole deal that being a parent brings to the picnic. Here are some tips from Emily, who has had a bash at this and met some nice men, though has not experienced much in the fireworks department via this method (so far!).

- Choose a site that matches you – no point going on a dating site hosted by a newspaper you'd never be seen dead reading. Browse the site and see if you find it easy to use, like its feel and the way it works.
- Smile in your photo – many people don't, probably because they think they look better if they don't. It might be technically true, but who feels like actively seeking out a miserable sod for a date? (Only another miserable sod, I suppose.)
- Sell yourself; make the most of your best attributes (e.g. have Grade 2 in piano). Feels shallow but everyone else is doing it too. Try and make it sound like you though, so do more than just the tick-box bit – write things, too.
- Be specific about the type of date you're after (e.g. age range, location). It's a ruthless business, but what you're doing is finding someone who ticks all the boxes in terms of age, location, etc., then you can meet and see if there's any chemistry. It's the reverse of what we usually do at parties, when you find someone you like and then discover they live 200 miles away. The Internet is very good at filtering those out, and rubbish at the chemistry bit, so play to its strengths and stick to your criteria.
- The people I speak to who enjoy the experience most and get most out of it are proactive. You can just post your profile and wait for someone to say they're interested, or, like one woman I met who signed up to one of the biggest sites, sit down with a gin and tonic and start searching. After four hours she'd found four that she liked the look of and emailed them telling them a bit more about herself. She and one of her chosen four ended up emailing each other every day for a month and then met up. I met her at the end of her first date, which must've gone well as this was about 1 a.m. and she'd met him earlier for lunch!
- Talk on the phone before you meet, but get their number. It means

you've got to make the call, which is a bit scary but at least if they're dogs they won't be able to phone you. A chat's important, as typing, rather than conversation, might be their forte.

- Don't give your home address or home phone number until you're sure they're genuine (remember there's a very fine line between being trusting and being naïve).

9 *Singles Holidays*

This one leaves Emily cold, as she'd hate to be cooped up with a load of single people. Kate, on the other hand, would think nothing of making for Agadir with a load of singles and a pile of books, believing that if there really was no one to befriend or hang out with over a sangria, then some sun, a pool and time away from the children to catch up on her reading would be most welcome.

10 *Personal Ads*

Kate and Emily go double-dating! Here is a little tale to recount about our experience thus far with the small ads!

A couple of years ago we were larking and chatting that we'd like to get out a bit more, stir up the pot and meet some new people and, who knows, maybe even end up with a peck on the cheek?! Rather than go out together and sit in a bar, where history has shown our pulling power to be v. poor (we're the only girls we know who have been to a 'meat market' and had a very pleasant evening chatting to each other with no interruptions), we thought we'd do proper dating and go together on blind dates. So the idea of double-dating was born. So what if we met a couple of prannies? We'd still have fun and, anyhow, there's safety in numbers. We also felt it was a good sign if our blind date had at least one friend, then he probably wouldn't be totally weird! Deciding where to put the ad was a bit of a nerve-jangler but we eventually decided to place it in the week-end *FT* – the theory being that they'd be more likely than readers of other papers to stump up for the bill. This is what the advert said:

'Trinny and Susannah looking for Ant and Dec. Failing that, Cannon and Ball will do. Meet for fun, food and laughs, London area ... – No funny business.'

We recorded our ad for the *FT*. I say 'we' recorded it, actually Kate did the talking and Emily pushed the buttons. It's a partnership that works: brains and brawn.

We asked for text alerts to Emily's phone. Number of times phone rang: 6. Number of dates we went on: 0.

First up were Cannon and Ball (not their real names). Cannon was in the driving seat on this one and made the introductory call from his car ('Bad suspension, buggers my back up but great fun' – i.e. 'natty sports car that I'm probably too old to drive'). He called from his 'portable phone' (think he was trying to be endearing rather than thick). In the space of about five minutes Cannon had told Emily:

- I've a yacht which I sail for four months of the year.
- The helicopter had to go after the divorce.
- My friend is much nicer than me and does IT.
- I'm staying at my friend's in Shropshire, my dog's going mad sniffing at the mice.
- Bloody cold here, so draughty even the mice freeze.
- Come for lunch (to Shropshire) we'll cook you venison, pheasant, etc. We've been shooting.
- Love a laugh – it's the food of life.
- You sound great fun. *(Please note, Emily had done nothing other than giggle pathetically.)*
- Have you got big tits?
- Never come to London, you come here, bring the children.
- You sound wonderful, funny and sexy.
- Which one of us do you fancy? You can say me, he won't be hurt.

It was at this point that Emily bailed out sharpish. Cannon and Ball were a jolly pair and would be the sort who would liven up an evening with a bit of lively banter, but Emily had one of those revelation moments: she likes meeting people socially where it's all so much gentler – you talk to people if you like them, and if you don't you can move away without causing any offence. The conversation was too much of a sales pitch and she felt like she had a great big sign on her head saying: 'FOR SALE OPEN TO ALL AND ANY OFFERS'.

So what's our advice on the small ads? Personally we'd rather do it on the Internet as the dating site can block emails from people who creep you off, and that's trickier with the small ads. In hindsight, the foursome idea probably over-fired the readers' imagination! Perhaps bin the double-dating idea!

11 *Dating Agencies*

Dating agencies cost money as they offer a personalized service, matching you with other singletons as well as organizing events, dinners and so on. On the plus side, agencies offer another brain on the case and involved in the mission as well as some hand-picked dates and a degree of filtering. On the negative side, they take up money and time, as you need to meet the matchmaker and share your personal information. For some punters the fact that they cost money is part of the attraction, because it means that whomever you meet is prepared to commit a decent amount to finding people like you. Kate joined one years ago and got more than her money's worth, though as she joined with a friend she had a bit of a poor attitude and spent a lot of time laughing at people (rather than with them) in a rather immature fashion! But as one of our friends who used a dating agency properly said, 'I didn't meet The One, but I did have a couple of lovely flings and made a great friend.' On the other hand, another one of our friends said, 'What a waste of money that was! I went out for a bev with a couple of short, old blokes!'

A little pep talk from the girls before you date

- Read the paper for a month before you go out so you know what's going on in the real world and the celebrity world of who's with whom and other 'important' world events. Read about new films out, etc. You'll be armed with conversation and feel like you've more to talk about than just children.

- Go and see a film, watch the TV programme or series of the moment, go to an exhibition – do anything that means you can talk about it, recommend it or discuss it with your date.

- Say when you're making arrangements for the date that you've an early start the next day (so true with children anyway!) and so you can't be out too late. Oh, the joys of having to get back to a babysitter who needs to go home when the date goes sour or just plain dull, eh?

- No more than three drinks (seriously!). And that includes the one you had before for Dutch courage! Any more and ANYONE will look good.

- Tell someone where you're going and make sure it's a public place.

- Be curious about people – ask lots of questions. Listen to the answers!

- Dress code, girls – it's legs or cleavage, not the double whammy (or quadruple whammy if you show all).

- Don't moan – you're out to have fun! In particular, keep any stories about your ex or how you came to be divorced/single, etc. to yourself. It's amazingly unattractive.

- Don't wear old grey undies. Even if they're not going to see them, a sneak preview of a grey bra-strap is a no-no. Good undergarments are also excellent for inner poise and confidence.

- Ladies – don't suggest a second date; that's his job. We don't care that it's well into the new millennium and you're a cabinet minister or run ICI. Just say, 'Thank you, I've had a lovely time,' and wait for him to take it further.

- Old rules still apply – no monkey business on the first date. Even if it's been years ...

Introducing Your New Man to the Children

So, you've hooked a man. A small co-parenting point here: if you've agreed to tell your children's father when you're going to be introducing new partners to the children, then time to tell him! If you haven't formally agreed it between you but you know you'd want him to tell you when he was going to be introducing a new girlfriend, then you should do the same for him.

Introduce your new partner to the children when you're reasonably confident that this relationship may be a runner. The most concerning thing about many partners is that the children may get attached and won't like it if too many people come and go in their lives. This doesn't mean that you should hide your new friend, but that the more meaningful integration shouldn't occur until you feel confident. As we say, 'Children one step behind.' Talk to the children, reinforcing the things that we mentioned earlier. This is not a replacement for Dad, this is an adult friend for them, and you still love them just as much and so on.

Start to bring him into conversation: 'I'm going to the pictures with a friend called Rudolph.' Then maybe when you get back, report an interesting snippet that you think your children might like to know, e.g. 'Rudolph can do the splits.' If they ask questions, be honest, but play the whole thing down. 'Yes, you may meet him some day, I'm just getting to know him and it takes a long time to see if you really like someone. I'll introduce you when I know he's nice.'

When it comes to the introductions, just remember to be sensitive to their feelings. Give the situation the best chance of success:

- Choose a time that is good for them, not when they're tired or hungry or would rather be at football or are missing a friend's birthday party.
- Meet somewhere neutral and keep it less than an hour.
- Remember that one reason you've got to let things develop at a slow and natural pace is that if you put pressure on the children to become friends with your new man, this can make them feel like they're being unfair and a traitor to their other parent. So be

gentle; children do have these amazing antennae! Kate clearly remembers bringing a love interest home for a drink and to meet the children. He could just as easily have been a colleague from work that they hadn't met for all they knew, but he wasn't and Kate desperately wanted it to go well! As if by magic the children knew it (aged three and five!). They came downstairs, took one look and ran back to bed, hiding under their duvets and refusing to be coaxed out – well, not until she said they could have a bag of crisps! Maybe it was something about the way Kate was being, whatever; the little tikes clock the difference between friend and love interest quickly!

Keep a very gentle pace for some while. This is important and, to recap: keep in mind that this has more to do with the following list of how the children feel, than with the relationship between you and Rudolph the gymnast:

- They're experiencing major change again.
- They may feel powerless to influence and just want to be noticed.
- They may be anxious, with loads of little niggles about how day-to-day life may change.
- They're having to let go of the fantasy that Mum and Dad will be reunited.
- There may be a feeling of loss, having to share their parent.
- They may feel what they interpret as a betrayal: that the happy little unit of them and Mum wasn't enough for you.
- In some shape or form they're likely to feel sad and/or angry.

They can get over all of this. Seeing this list written out may help you realize that it can be a lot for them to take on board, but also that all of these concerns are surmountable with lots of talking and reassurance. Let them know that you understand that they may be feeling some of these things. Let them know that it's all right, and demonstrate your willingness to listen. When a child is hostile to someone new, try to find out why. Ask questions that will enable them to describe what it is they're uncomfortable with. Take anything they say seriously.

Helping the children get to know him properly

As things become more serious, do keep talking, and talking, to the children and remember that they need lots of reassurance and little signs that everything is still OK and will be fine. Although you may believe that the children are part of the package, and as a consequence part of their mother, in one respect they are and in another they're not. They're individuals whose relationship with every new person needs to develop at its own pace, so give it time.

Lots of everyday stuff like eating together, playing games, hanging out, going for walks, kicking a football about will help. Make sure there's still a quantity of time without your boyfriend around, and make sure the children know they'll not be doing everything with you in couple mode. The best thing you can do at the outset is to give it time … don't force it. Here are some ideas that might work as you get to know each other better.

If you help the children cope and manage this change in their lives, a new partner can be great. The children can get on and do their own thing without worrying about you. Children may feel responsible for your happiness, so you having a boyfriend can be a good thing by relieving them, to some extent, of this burden. If you've chosen wisely, the children will have not only another good source of love, friendship and support in their lives, they will have another good male role model. They will also be witnessing all the ins and outs, gives and takes, ups and downs that are part and parcel of a good and functioning adult romantic partnership.

Dos and don'ts for you and your new man

We've included this as the major lesson that Kate has learned is that when you're at an early stage in your relationship and you want it to go well, you don't want to be fussing or always saying 'Do this' and 'Don't do that.' The end result is that you just hope it'll all be OK. We think this marvellous list of dos and don'ts can really give a new boyfriend a helping hand in getting it right, and it can save you from stressing that you really should say something to him about it. We believe that looking at this, and showing this page to someone who probably doesn't really know how to get it right, can give your relationship a better chance. So go on … read, think and share!

- Remember, your home is your child's home too, and just as you would expect your child to respect any guest, your new partner should behave respectfully towards your child.
- This means that your new partner should NOT …
  - tease your child
  - correct or discipline him, except when there's clear or significant danger
  - call your children nicknames they don't like (or even ones they do like if your new man hasn't been 'invited' to do so)
  - pry, interfere or offer unsolicited advice about anything (even if it's well-meaning)
  - enter their room or private space without an invitation
  - join in an activity or conversation without having been specifically invited by you or your child
  - touch or interact with your child in any way that the child finds uncomfortable, no matter how innocent it is – including play fights, rough and tumble, tickling, etc.
  - mention to the child anything you've discussed about the child ('Your mum told me about the argument you had,' or 'I gather you're not enjoying school at the moment.')
  - attempt to coerce your children into doing anything they don't want to do
  - compete for love and attention. The love for a partner is so wholly different to the love for the children that conflict really shouldn't be allowed to arise.

But he SHOULD do these ...

- decide in his own mind how he'd like his role to develop: a special grown-up pal, a confidant they can turn to, a mentor to guide them, a guardian angel godparent style, a coach?
- let the relationship develop gently over time. He should try and think of someone from his childhood he had a special friendship with as a child.
- try not to be desperate. He may be head over heels with Mum and keen to make a good impression, but to the children this doesn't make a bean of difference. Trying too hard may backfire badly.
- remember that it's likely that they will kick off and take against him from the start. He should try to be as relaxed as possible about this. He shouldn't feel a failure because they don't like him straight off. This in all probability is not about HIM. He needs to try to keep detached and cool.
- make it perfectly clear that he's not the dad when meeting people with the children who don't realize. (This is one from Kate's children.)
- make it clear from everything he does and says that he has no intention of getting in the way of their relationship with their mum or dad. Keep well outside the parent/child zone.
- remember he's the grown-up and that one day (soon!) the children will grow up and realize that he's fine and that their relationship with him can be good and positive for all. It may take a while but don't fret, don't push and don't pressurize.

Dear Reader,

We hope that some of what we have passed on from our own experiences and from all the people we have met has helped you to digest the past, to see a way forward and how to give your children a fair crack at a happy childhood. We hope too that you're beginning to feel a frisson of excitement about your own future!

Good luck, and in the words of Mark Twain:

> " Twenty years from now you will be more disappointed by the things that you didn't do than by the things you did do, so throw off the bowlines. Sail away from the safe harbor. Catch the trade winds in your sails. Explore. Dream. Discover. "

Love, Kate and Emily

SERIOUS RESOURCES

Kate and Emily   www.kateandemily.com

One Parent Families   www.oneparentfamilies.org.uk;
/Gingerbread   www.gingerbread.org.uk
                               08000185026

Relate   www.relate.org.uk
                               01788573241

Family Mediators Assoc   www.familymediators.co.uk
                               02078819400

National Family Mediation   www.nfm.u-net.com
                               02074858809

British Association for Counselling
and Psychotherapy   www.bacp.co.uk
                               08704435252

Families Need Fathers   www.fnf.org.uk
                               02076135060

National Association of Child www.nacc.org.uk
Contact Centres   08707703269

Collaborative law	www.collablaw.co.uk
Resolution, advice re collaborative law	www.resolution.org.uk 0168920272

Financial help and advice / money-making-wheezes sites

Martin Lewis's free financial advice site	www.moneysavingexpert.com
Citizens Advice Bureau	www.citizensadvice.org.uk
Find out what benefits you're entitled to	www.entitledto.com
Find an Independent Financial Advisor (IFA)	www.unbiased.co.uk
Get free help and advice about CVs, training, careers and courses	www.learndirect-advice.co.uk

Here are some websites with ideas and details of fun things for you and your family to get into. If anything grabs your fancy, get on the phone or on the web to find out what's on offer ... more than you can ever have imagined!

Library locator	www.findyourlibrary.co.uk
Youth Hostelling Association	www.yha.org.uk 08707708868

Ideas for days out

A picnic locator	www.allkids.co.uk
Love films DVD hire	www.lovefilm.com
Find a campsite	www.find-a-campsite.co.uk
Find adult education	www.hotcourses.com
Single parent holidays	www.smallfamilies.co.uk 01763226567
WI (not just jam and Jerusalem)	www.womens-institute.co.uk 02073719300
Wildlife Trust	www.wildlifetrusts.org
Rambling club	www.ramblers.org 02073398500
Friends Reunited	www.friendsreunited.co.uk
Weight Watchers	www.weightwatchers.co.uk
Creative writing	www.creativewritingonline.co.uk
Charity work	www.timebank.org.uk 08454561668
Crisis at Christmas	www.crisis.org.uk 0844251011
Find a choir to join	www.choirs.org.uk
Find a local dance class	www.danceweb.co.uk

We hope you enjoyed this Hay House book.
If you would like to receive a free catalogue featuring additional
Hay House books and products, or if you would like information
about the Hay Foundation, please contact:

Hay House UK Ltd
292B Kensal Rd • London W10 5BE
Tel: (44) 20 8962 1230; Fax: (44) 20 8962 1239
www.hayhouse.co.uk

✳✳✳

Published and distributed in the United States of America by:
Hay House, Inc. • PO Box 5100 • Carlsbad, CA 92018-5100
Tel.: (1) 760 431 7695 or (1) 800 654 5126;
Fax: (1) 760 431 6948 or (1) 800 650 5115
www.hayhouse.com

Published and distributed in Australia by:
Hay House Australia Ltd • 18/36 Ralph St • Alexandria NSW 2015
Tel.: (61) 2 9669 4299; Fax: (61) 2 9669 4144
www.hayhouse.com.au

Published and distributed in the Republic of South Africa by:
Hay House SA (Pty) Ltd • PO Box 990 • Witkoppen 2068
Tel./Fax: (27) 11 467 8904 • www.hayhouse.co.za

Published and distributed in India by:
Hay House Publishers India • Muskaan Complex • Plot No.3
B-2 • Vasant Kunj • New Delhi – 110 070.
Tel.: (91) 11 41761620; Fax: (91) 11 41761630.
www.hayhouse.co.in

Distributed in Canada by:
Raincoast • 9050 Shaughnessy St • Vancouver, BC V6P 6E5
Tel.: (1) 604 323 7100; Fax: (1) 604 323 2600

✳✳✳

Sign up via the Hay House UK website to receive the Hay House
online newsletter and stay informed about what's going on with
your favourite authors. You'll receive bimonthly announcements
about discounts and offers, special events, product highlights,
free excerpts, giveaways, and more!
www.hayhouse.co.uk